the little book of
MORE

the evolution of YOU

Lynda Reid, EdD, PCC

BALBOA.
PRESS
A DIVISION OF HAY HOUSE

Balboa Press books may be ordered through booksellers or by contacting:

Balboa Press
A Division of Hay House
1663 Liberty Drive
Bloomington, IN 47403
www.balboapress.com
1 (877) 407-4847

Print information available on the last page.

ISBN: 978-1-9822-0876-9 (sc)
ISBN: 978-1-9822-0878-3 (hc)
ISBN: 978-1-9822-0877-6 (e)

Library of Congress Control Number: 2018908583

Balboa Press rev. date: 08/15/2018

To my mother, Lois, for inspiring me to be MORE.
To my husband, Ali, thank you for your unconditional
love and never-ending support. You have
helped expand my life and my potential.

Table of Contents

Preface

The concept of MORE was born from my own life's journey. My journey has been filled with intentional and unintentional teachers, who have stretched my thinking, expanded my awareness, and deepened my understanding of my sense of self.

As a lifelong educator, I have always sought out and applied the latest in neuroscience research to my teaching and to my life. The research informed and expanded my understanding of how we learn, change, and foster positive learning and growth. Choosing to live and work outside of my home culture and country of Alberta, Canada, deepened my understanding of myself. The experiences inspired my master's and doctoral research on the importance of cultural immersion for expanding our sense of self and fostering opportunities to understand and embrace diversity.

My personal journey and the experiences of my students and coaching clients have assisted me in clarifying and articulating the core elements and components inherent within MORE. I weave our collective stories throughout the book to trigger connections to your own life's journey and stimulate your process of growth and evolution.

My work has been heavily influenced and inspired by the research and work of a host of great minds. A list of reference suggestions is included at the end, for those who wish to explore similar concepts of MORE through the work and guidance of other leaders in the field.

MORE is how I strive to live my life; it is my compass, leading me forward and reminding me where and when I go astray. I offer MORE to you as a simple tool for guiding you forward; ever evolving and expanding your potential.

It is important to note that your brain has developed its neuropathways and habits throughout your life and always follows the road "most" travelled. Neuroscience has demonstrated that our brains need months of continual positive reinforcement to create a new habit and pattern of thought. MORE requires patience and a focus on every small step forward.

Acknowledgments

There are no individual successes. Every success has involved the input and support of others. The creation and writing of MORE is a result of contributions from numerous people.

Thank you to my initial readers, Johnette Hartnett, Karlene Chorney, Sheilagh O'Dwyer, Paul McGinniss, Ginger Vieira, and Alan Stracke, for their thoughtful insights and questions that stretched my thinking and writing.

Thank you to Genny Wright-Hailey for her editing, critique, patience, and persistence in honing my thoughts and words and to the editors at Balboa Press for their input and final polish of my work. Special thank you to Lincoln Dwyer for being my go to, on call and creative graphic designer.

Thank you to my family, friends, students, and clients whose lives and experiences have inspired me to create and share the concept of MORE with a broader audience.

Introduction

Are you living your potential or just getting by in the repetitive numbness of good enough? This book explores four core elements that are essential tools for moving you beyond your current limitations to expanding your full potential.

Welcome to *The Little Book of MORE: The Evolution of YOU.* Congratulations on taking another step forward in your process by selecting a book that will stretch your thinking, support your growth, and celebrate your accomplishments. MORE develops holistically, fostering a richness that is centered at your core, challenging your habitual patterns and leading you forward toward owning and living your potential. Actively seeking to create MORE will provide you with the capabilities to create a life centered on the continuous development of health, happiness, and contentment in all that you do.

MORE's four core elements—meaning, owning, relationships, and emotions— demand your dedication to moving beyond your status quo, to accept that harmony and fulfillment are possible in your life and that you have the power and opportunity to create them. Although the core elements fall into the order of the acronym, they do not form a linear process. As you work to fully embed and nurture MORE in your daily interactions and decisions, you move across all the core elements, weaving them into an upward spiral that will guide your way of being, interacting, and believing.

This book takes you on a journey through each core element. We will explore the creation of *meaning*, examine how to *own* your potential, gain clarity on fostering *relationships*, and discover respect for all *emotions*.

MORE requires you to fully engage in the process of living. MORE is a way of believing and interacting. It is built on how you create meaning, own your potential, foster relationships, and understand and respect emotions. The MORE is a commitment to yourself—to honoring your worth, abilities, and potential. MORE builds on your strengths, supports and fosters your growth, and turns your failures into opportunities for learning and success. It requires your honest acceptance of where you are and where you wish to go. The MORE process acknowledges that growth toward your potential is never easy, usually messy, and continually challenging. MORE requires a commitment to your positive growth and potential, and patience to allow your life to develop over time.

Meaning

Owning

Relationships

Emotions

Blog Post: Remember When

Do you remember your first best friend? The one you played with for hours on end, the one you told secrets to and trusted with your fears, the one who was your partner in all your childhood explorations?

My best friend was Karen. Her family moved in down the street when we were both four years old. We were inseparable through most of our school years. Growing up before the need for playdates and physical boundaries, Karen and I explored the reaches of our neighborhood and the country roads that began at the end of our block. The older we got, the braver we became and the further we explored. We were Huck Finn and Tom Sawyer; we were runaways and adventurers. We packed lunches, hopped on our little coaster bikes, and explored for hours. Our backyards became tented escapes, penny carnivals, and a wide array of locations for escapades and characters. We rode the city buses to swimming lessons, art classes, and Saturday afternoon matinees. Our sleepovers involved little sleep and a lot of talking. We laughed, we learned, and we cried together. We believed anything was possible. The Disney movie *Peter Pan* inspired us to become scientists as we endeavored to create pixie dust. Perhaps we just didn't get the right combination of the white, sprinkly substances—flour, sugar, and salt? Undaunted, we continued to believe that, just like our Barbies, we could do anything.

Our lives have taken us in very different directions and led us down very different paths, but always, we will be part of each other—the part that believes we can be MORE.

Lynda Reid, EdD, PCC

From Passive to Active MORE

As a child, I had no idea how hard my parents worked to make ends meet and give my two sisters and me all that we had. We never seemed to lack anything. I had friends who had more things and friends who had less, but we all appeared to have enough. We lived the epitome of 1950s and '60s middle-class Canada. The economy grew, wages rose, and everyone began to need, buy, and collect more of everything.

I grew up a shopper. In Edmonton, Alberta, everyone knew the location of every high school by its adjacent mall. As a young adult, I purchased as I wished, never stopping to pay attention to the motivation behind my purchases. Buying made me feel good; it was such a rewarding experience that I ignored my ever-increasing credit card debt. Consumerism fed my ego and gave me an artificial, passive, outside-in sense of worth.

It was not until I chose to move to the British Virgin Islands (BVI) that I forced myself to deal with my debt. I arrived in the Caribbean debt free. I soon learned that my meager savings in Canadian dollars turned into next to nothing in the US-dollar-based currency used in the BVI. That, combined with the minimum salary I received teaching at a small private school, threw me into a new understanding and appreciation of what I needed. I began to examine how I could essentially have MORE by living with less. It forced—or should I say *allowed?*—me to actively explore my worth from the inside out, not the outside in.

Meaning

Owning

Relationships

Emotions

belonging
passion
purpose
loss

Blog Post: The Jump Rope Syndrome

"Not last night, but the night before …" we seven-year-olds sing as I jump in rhythm to the skipping rope. "Twenty-four robbers came knocking at my door." I mime knocking as I continue to jump. "I went out … " Breathless, I jump away from the rope, race around my best friend's back, and prepare to jump back into the skipping rope's rhythm as we continue, "While they went … *in!*" I jump back into the rhythm just as the recess bell pierces the din of our childhood freedom.

There was always a tension between the anticipation of the jump into the swinging rope and actually jumping. When it came to double Dutch (jumping into two alternating skipping ropes) the tension could easily be paralyzing. Once you successfully jumped in, the longer you were able to navigate the rhythm of the rope, the more excited you felt and the more satisfying the experience. But what if you had to jump the rope, had to stay in, and had to keep singing the same song over and over?

Many of us live our lives in the rhythm of our own jump-rope games. We know the song, the players, the actions—going to work, taking care of family, controlling finances, and managing home, health, and day-to-day necessities. Initially, each of those jump-rope games excited us, inspired us, and challenged us to explore and expand who we were and who we could become. So at what point did we transition from excited into complacent? When did we become numb to the endless repetition of our lives, paralyzed in our repetition? How did we decide that this is all that there is and good enough? Why do we allow ourselves to live without passion or purpose and settle for less than our dreams?

It doesn't have to be this way. We can move beyond complacency and repetition. We can reconnect with and actualize passion and purpose in our lives. We can create *meaning* in our lives.

Meaning

MORE's core element of *meaning* acknowledges our need to belong, contribute, and play a part in creating a greater purpose. Meaning and purpose are not given to us but are what we create from all that is given. They are found in living our lives passionately, accepting the wisdom that comes from our challenges, and spreading kindness in the darkest of corners.

Many of us live overwhelmed in today's always-on culture. The yin and yang of technology allow us the freedom to work from anywhere and yet restrict our ability to let go, reflect, process, and revive. Taxed to the maximum, we have lost our sense of human beings, exceeded our lives as human doings, and now multitask like human viruses, causing much of the imbalance, dis-ease, and disease in our lives. In our viral state of multitasking and simultaneously attempting to control all the multiple aspects of our lives, we lose sight of our bigger pictures, our purposes, and what truly gives meaning and value to our lives.

We live in numbness; a state of being overwhelmed clouds our ability to seek and create meaning. Asking for help may feel pointless—just a continuation of the same cycle. Always tethered to technology, we can feel isolated and disconnected from others and ourselves. We stay in relationships and jobs that do not serve us, creating toxic environments that breed the *dis-ease to disease* cycle in our lives, the cycle that feeds a nagging cough, another cold, an unexplained rash, stiff joints, the sleepless nights—you know your list. Many of us carry on blindly or blatantly ignoring the dysfunction in which we exist. Prolonged high stress keeps our brains functioning in a threat state, which limits our abilities to problem-solve our way through daily dilemmas, blocks our creativity and insight, and starves our ability to communicate clearly. We live in sleep deprivation, manage our lives with medications (prescription and nonprescription), and create toxic cellular conditions that lead to heart attack, stroke, and other stress-related diseases. This clouded, caustic way of being builds barriers between you, your loved ones, and your meaning. When your life lacks meaning, you feel trapped, depressed, and worthless.

> Even a rewarding career can become caustic when you find yourself living in a prolonged high-stress state. For instance, Thomas's work environment trapped him between fulfillment and frustration. While he found great professional satisfaction in working directly with his customers, the office environment was toxic. Struggling to survive, Thomas disappeared within his headset, immersed in the sanctuary of his music, which shielded him from his colleagues' negativity. Striving to continually meet his clients' needs, he found solace after hours in the quiet of the empty office. Exhausted and sleep deprived, Thomas found that the sense of meaning he gained with his clients was overshadowed and diminished by the realities of his work environment.

The dysfunction in Thomas's workplace robbed him of a sense of belonging and meaning and created toxic stress in his life. Long-term stress is insidious; it slowly strangles your connection to others and barricades you behind walls of exhaustion and apathy, hijacking your connection to your meaning.

Long-term and extreme stress can partner with other major life situations, such as poor health, aging parents, divorce, job loss, and negative relationships, each of which can send you spiraling into a pit of meaninglessness. Striving to balance the stresses with the day-to-day demands of living can be all-consuming, obscuring our sense of meaning and purpose.

You may be one of the people sandwiched between aging parents, a growing family, and your career, just like my client Sofia. She felt stressed and torn between the demands of her career, the health and daily needs of her aging parents, quality time with her children, and supportive time with her spouse. She lived in a continual state of feeling overwhelmed. Spread thin among the multitude of competing demands, she felt hollow, completely disconnected from her meaning. Near breakdown, Sofia finally realized she needed help. She chose to ask her siblings to step up and assist with their parents. Working through her siblings' excuses and resistance took effort. They were able to create a plan that lifted the sole burden of her parents' needs off her shoulders. She has room to breathe, enjoy her children, connect with her spouse, succeed professionally, and appreciate the time she spends with her parents.

The ever-changing career landscape can stretch our sense of purpose and potential to the breaking point. You may be one of the millions who were laid off, struggling to be recognized and hired for your talents and experience as you attempt to navigate the increasingly impersonal hiring practices of online applications.

Julian is an amazingly talented marketing and communications professional who has had to take on a variety of secondary jobs to pay his bills and live day-to-day. Even once hired, he has found, as newest hire, he is the first to be let go. As his longing to belong, to contribute, to be part of a greater good was ignored, his spirit deadened along with his desire for meaning. Julian came to coaching desperate for a new way forward. As he moved past his roadblocks and barriers, he opened his thoughts to new possibilities and alternative avenues to explore. He registered for adult continuing education courses to update and enhance his degree and expertise. Julian's new learning led to new professional connections and a wider range of career opportunities. New purpose and passions reignited meaning in his life.

Even a company's new direction or new upper management hire can derail our lives and sense of meaning. I thought I held my personal and professional life together through my husband's cancer, bone marrow transplant, and recovery. A new organizational direction and the increasing demands of my professional role created an incredibly stressful environment that continually stretched my abilities, depleting the meaning I had gained from my work. I felt micromanaged, manipulated, overwhelmed, and publicly ridiculed. Sleep was fleeting and rarely sustaining. I ate for comfort, gained weight, and self-medicated with many glasses of wine each evening. It was not until I was driving home from work after a performance review fearful and concerned about how I was going to tell my husband, who was still recovery from a bone marrow transplant, that I no longer had a job, that it hit me: *I'm free! I am free to pursue and do just what I am meant to do.* Just what that was didn't strike me immediately, but the elation of the freedom was immense and helped carry me through the beginning of my transition to reconnect me with meaning in my life.

All my coaching clients have spent decades feeling as though their stress buttons are permanently switched on, as their jobs and life events require them to respond to and be ready for crisis and disaster at any moment. Meaning and purpose are lost, as survival seems all-consuming. It is at these moments of overwhelm and frustration that we can find our greatest opportunities for creating and living with meaning.

When you seek to embrace MORE in your life, you will begin to find meaning in all that you do. Living with meaning allows you to create harmony between your work life and your personal life, integrating the two with purpose and intent. You will begin to intentionally seek out opportunities that will expand meaning in your personal and professional life. Meaning will evolve naturally as you actively foster belonging, embrace your passions, and live your purpose. Meaning making is a transformational experience and expands for us as we seek to create meaning through loss, hardship, and even death.

Meaning through Belonging

For many of us, meaning in our lives is born through our connections with others. How we perceive our roles within our families, amongst our friends, and in relation to our colleagues creates meaning in our lives. Changing jobs, moving to a new location, a death of a family member, loss of friendship, or isolation from our peers can easily cause us to collapse, sending us down a negative spiral of defeat and worthlessness.

I never understood the importance belonging played in my life until I moved away from home, away from my family, my friends, and the country of my birth. Transitioning from Canada to the British Virgin Islands required more than an adjustment to climate and culture. I was no longer a visitor, a welcomed tourist; I was a Non-Belonger (the legal term used for expatriates at the time). I had to seek out new connections and create friendships within a small and closed culture. I learned that belonging was an active process that required me to move out of my cultural comfort zone, open up to others, and create new avenues for connecting. Risking isolation and rejection was the only way forward.

I was an unknown entity on the island, a teacher with no status. My move was just before the global commonality of broadband connectivity. There was no e-mail, Facebook, or Skype to instantly connect me back home. I could not afford a landline telephone in my home, so if I wanted to call home, I headed out for the pay phone. With no public transport on the island, I stood on the side of the road each morning to hitch to school. I initially felt undervalued and invisible. I had to find ways to prove my worth to others. I made mistakes, made assumptions, and created power struggles. I had to learn to let go, to listen honestly, and to genuinely show respect. Every day and every relationship provided opportunities to practice belonging. It was a voyage in making meaning.

> Dewain did not have to leave his country or even his home to experience feeling as isolated and undervalued as I had. He felt it every day he went to work. Ironically, his isolation came from the open office cubicle environment in which he worked. Dewain felt closed off from his coworkers by barriers of negativity and distrust that might just as well have been concrete walls.

> Through the coaching process, Dewain explored ideas for reconnecting and consciously attempting to shift the closed, negative energy in the office to a more open and inclusive community of colleagues. He deliberately thanked and complimented his colleagues, showed interest in their families and activities, and suggested ways they could create a more fun and engaged environment in the office. His attempts to raise the positive energy of the office environment were rejected or dismissed. People were too busy to chat, and no one wanted anything to do with having fun at work. His closest colleague told him, "Look, Dewain, I

just want to do my projects and get out of here." With every affirmative action Dewain employed, he became more and more frustrated. As he reflected and shared his frustration, an insight occurred. The invisible walls served as protection against the negativity of their toxic leader. Self-survival trumped all. His colleagues found comfort and safety within their negative cocoons. The positive change he desired was impossible, out of his control.

As Dewain processed his insights, he came to the realization that staying in the toxic work environment was detrimental to his mental and physical health. The only thing in his control was his ability to let go and move on. The risk of leaving the job became less than staying within the job. Dewain began to plan, network, and seek other employment opportunities. Even before he landed his new job, Dewain began to experience a sense of freedom and optimism for creating a new place for belonging. Through the freedom to move forward, Dewain began to rebuild meaning in his life.

A strong sense of belonging in our workplace provides meaning in our lives. We feel connected to our coworkers and take pride in our organization. It's when you describe your company's actions and policies with the pronoun *we*. Those of us who feel that pride in belonging, especially when we are supported in our professional growth, often desire to achieve more and move up our professional ladder, expanding meaning in our lives.

Catherine is one such person. She gained a great sense of meaning in her job. She felt part of a great corporate mission, part of the team. Catherine's career moved forward when she achieved a long-sought-after promotion. She was now in the leadership position she had worked so hard to attain.

"This is going to be easy," she had confidently stated during our first coaching session. Promoted from within, she knew the company, knew the client needs and challenges, and had a clear vision for taking her team to the next level. She flew into her new role with great enthusiasm. She knew now was the time to make change happen.

By our second coaching session, Catherine's confidence was waning. She felt resistance and negativity from her former coworkers. Rather than accepting, supporting and cheering her on, as they always had, they now were questioning and critical. "I don't understand it. I feel such great resistance. Joanne is passive-aggressive, and I've caught Mark and Janice exchanging eye rolls and snickering at my comments."

In the safe space of the coaching conversation, Catherine processed her feelings and reflected on the actions of her now direct reports. She was able to step back from her change agenda and the microcosm of daily interactions. Catherine's perspective shifted, allowing her to see how her new role and ideas were impacting others. She recognized the threat her change of position placed on her team and the range of emotions it triggered. Some were fearful of her new ideas, a few felt betrayed by her desire to lead, and one in particular, Catherine realized, was full of envy. With these recognitions, Catherine knew she needed to form a new sense of belonging and improve relational connections to calm the fear-based emotional reactions. Formulating a structured team-coaching plan provided her an avenue to actively build meaningful interactions, empower the strengths that resided in her team, and create a new culture of mutual support and acceptance. By demonstrating that she still respected and needed others, she revitalized and bonded everyone into a new sense of team, belonging, and meaning.

Many leaders often assume that belonging happens naturally, without conscious effort, and that once it is there, it will always be there. Just as Catherine realized, belonging is an active, ongoing process that creates connections, commitment, and meaning for one's employees. Meaning through belonging becomes even more challenging to create in the anonymity of today's online-based work environment.

Bianca works from the comfort of her home, coordinating her clients' needs. Her limited face-to-face interactions with her national colleagues are spread out throughout the year. Initially, the ability to work from home gave her a sense of freedom and empowerment. It was not until her relationship with her spouse began to deteriorate that she felt the isolation of the combination of her work and her home environment. While changing her work environment was impossible without changing jobs, Bianca began to explore how she could branch out beyond her home and create new connections and a sense of belonging.

For Bianca, belonging came as she reconnected with her spiritual needs and joined a church. She invited her husband to attend with her. Together, they relished the new sense of belonging they felt in the church community. Bianca felt a renewed connection with her husband. The strengthening of her marriage and her new sense of community validated her as a person and fostered a new sense of meaning in her life.

Our life partners and families play an integral part in our ability to create a sense of belonging and meaning in our lives. Meaning in my life shattered when my first husband informed me, "At the end of the month, either you could move or I will." My life, sense of belonging, and meaning broke into disjointed and insignificant fragments. I lived in a fog, numb to all emotion. It was months before the two of us agreed to seek out counseling. Through my individual counseling sessions, I realized that my relationship had run its course.

Making the decision to divorce my first husband was the hardest decision I had ever made in my life. While I recognized that we had grown into people who no longer shared similar desires and goals, I had to deal with feelings of failure and self-worth. I went into my marriage "knowing" that I was never going to be one of those divorced people. I dealt with my feelings by blocking the idea of failure, using blame as a buffer and an excuse. I still had to grieve, process the loss, and begin my healing. Healing required I begin my first inward journey through all the components of MORE, traveling with all the baggage I had acquired in my twenty-seven years on this planet.

I was drawn to the wisdom within self-help books and was blessed to have a close girlfriend with whom to process the information and learn how to apply insights to my life. I felt as though I had found a new home, a place, and a mind-set in which to belong. This new empowering mind-set brought meaning to my life that fostered my connections to passion and purpose.

Meaning and Passion

My newfound belonging propelled and supported me to explore and pursue my passions. The more I immersed myself in things that I was passionate about, the more my energy increased, time expanded and insights became abundant. Many of my clients seek out coaching to prompt, explore, and develop their passions. Others come to me feeling passionless, devoid of all meaning. Their sense of overwhelm seems insurmountable, leading them to retreat to a robotic life of routine immersed in mediocrity.

As a coach, I seek to gently guide my clients to imagine their best possible lives personally and professionally. I ask what feeds their spirits, what excites and energizes them. Some just return blank stares, almost unable to process the possibility, let alone the words. Others immediately state that they have no idea, almost indignant at my asking. A few have crumbled into tears overwhelmed by hopelessness and despair. Over time, with patience and compassion, the questions begin to move their minds from the always-on threat state of "fight or flight" into a forward state of creative possibilities. Small steps lead to new horizons where the possibility of living life passionately can be not only seen but also actualized.

> "It's just a pipe dream," Ari replied during our first Skype coaching conversation. I always use session one for goal clarification, asking my clients to envision their goals as a current reality. Her "pipe dream" was the detailed description she had just given of how she would like to live her ultimate life. "I'm going to be forty years old. It's too late," she sighed in resignation.

> I paused, allowing the weight of her statement to settle in. "But what if it wasn't too late? What would you do?" After a bit of time stumbling through her

usual excuses, she began to open her thinking up to moving beyond her mental blockades and conditioned reasons. Her energy shifted, and she giggled as her mind opened to insights and opportunities for moving forward. She took control, stepping beyond her excuses and into her transition zone with passion as her guide.

Passion is our energy source. The more we connect and live with our passions, the more energy and excitement we can create in our lives. The more energy and excitement, the more meaning.

> Outwardly Roberto's life looked guided by his passions. His life appeared under control. His jovial persona seemingly fueled by passion: a successful career, respected position, great social life—"Living the thirty-something dream," he stated in our first coaching session. The façade began to fall away as my questions pushed him to dig deep and explore his goals and what gave meaning to his life. His cocky self-confidence melted away as he revealed that hidden within the lockbox of his desires was the completion of a novel. A book that had already begun to take form and substance had been halted a year before by self-doubt and the busyness of life. Once he acknowledged this insight and recognized his excuses had created the barriers, he began to create actions that moved him past his obstacles and self-doubt. He made time each day to embrace his writing. Reconnecting with his characters gave form and energy that rekindled his passion. Breathing life back into characters brought a rebirth of meaning to his life.

Even when your work centers on your passion and your career is all about meaning-making, events can challenge and derail your progress. Your health, a family issue, or a situation with coworkers can each stretch your ability to remain passionate about your career.

Cynthia's life is all about meaning. She is a visionary, a change agent and social advocate. Her research led her to create an organization comprised of a collection of self-managed social advocacy projects. While the vision was reliable and viable for some of the projects, one, in particular, was imploding. Personnel issues within the project drew Cynthia into the mix. She found herself "babysitting" the team, her time hijacked by the team's dysfunction. Gone was the time for her to pursue her vision and the development of bigger projects.

When we began working together, Cynthia was near complete breakdown; she resented the project, the employees, and their needs; she was ready to walk away. As she explored her options aloud, it was clear that walking away was not an option. Her passion and purpose were at the core of her organization and its greater potential. Over the weeks, clarity and options began to evolve. Events began to slowly unfold, freeing Cynthia to seek and create new opportunities that would lead her mission, her vision, and the struggling team forward into a new dynamic, supportive, and sustainable organization.

Reconnecting with your passions requires you to pause, reflect, and own your desires. Passions thought dead or out of reach can return, clarify, and take on new life. Just as Roberto allowed himself to embrace his passion for writing and Cynthia created new opportunities for moving her vision forward, so have others found their way to new careers, new locations, and new, fulfilling relationships. The essential pieces are your ability to open yourself to new possibilities and your willingness to challenge your assumptions and habits. Then listen. Make meaning through acknowledging your passions, creating space to explore them, and taking a series of continuous actions that transition them from whispers to reality.

Meaning and Purpose

While passion feeds the core of our being, purpose gives form and meaning to all that is given to us. Purpose makes things matter. Purpose allows us to learn, grow, and support others. We can create purpose through our careers, our families, our passions, and our interests. Purpose gives meaning.

The need to create meaning in my life began to clarify for me about seven years post-divorce from my first husband. I was on a highly successful career path toward public school leadership. I had already taught at every level (elementary through secondary) and had served as a consultant for the large city school board. The next natural step would be seeking an assistant principal position, which would lead to becoming a principal, but a long-held belief nagged at me. I had always believed that I was meant to live and work in another country, so why was I still in the city of my birth?

The thought of moving away from the safety and security of my successful personal and professional bubble was scary and daunting. I had already traveled through Europe, Mexico, Guatemala, and Belize. I had taken two extended trips to Australia and numerous vacations in the British Virgin Islands (BVI). When I began to seriously consider the possibility of moving to another country, the only place I could visualize myself living was the BVI. It was more than the stunning scenery and beautiful beaches; I felt truly drawn and connected to the culture and the people. The idea of living and working within the BVI community quieted the scary, daunting feelings; it felt safe, tranquil, and doable.

Using my spring break and contacts I had on the island, I found work at a small, evolving private school in Tortola, took the leap, and moved. Completely on my own, without friends or family, I became an active participant in creating meaning, actively seeking to weave purpose between my work and personal life.

> Weaving purpose and passion together came naturally for Trin, driving her professional goals and mission. Through her work, she lives her passions and her purpose, dedicated to her community and her people. She uses every job as an opportunity to enhance life for others. Trin is a nonprofit champion, a community advocate and change agent within her society. Meaning draws her forward, motivates her actions, and inspires her to reach for greater goals for the greater good. For Trin, passion and purpose weave seamlessly into the tapestry of meaning in her life.
>
> Unlike Trin, Connie's passion and purpose do not work as the warp and woof of a unique tapestry. Her passions and purpose weave two different yet magnificent tapestries, one of passion and one of purpose. Connie has moved through a series of exciting and engaging careers. Her work has connected her with individuals of influence and wealth from around the world. While her work fed her passion for adventure and excitement, she felt it lacked in purpose. Purpose for Connie is about giving back, championing those in need, and empowering individuals to move their lives forward. Connie has actualized her sense of purpose in the creation of a children's foundation and mission work

in Africa with her church. Connie's careers feed her passion; her purpose feeds her core and her meaning.

Our purpose is fed by all of our life experiences. As we evolve and our life stories unfold, we gain greater opportunities and experiences from which to create our purpose. Those of you with rich, fulfilling careers can find yourselves frozen and fearful as you approach retirement.

Tricia contacted me for coaching support to assist her in preparing for her transition into retirement. She felt very conflicted about the change. Tricia loved her career and was known as one of the best in her field. She pondered and dwelt on many questions: "What will happen to my clients once I leave? Who could do as much as I do for them?"

Tricia's husband was determined never to retire. "He will die doing what he loves," she stated with a sigh. He and their daughter told her repeatedly, "If you stop working, you'll die." Their comments fed her retirement fears. Retirement was an unknown, a void in which she would disappear.

Her self-doubt took the form of suffocating, relentless mental turmoil that robbed her of energy and insights. Her mind raced with questions: "If I leave, what will I do with all of my time? Who will do things with me? How will we pay our bills?" She wanted to let go; she knew it was time for someone to step into her role, someone with a new energy and a renewed sense of passion. She was frozen in indecision and fear.

Over the course of our coaching engagement, Tricia's insights led her to realize that not only could she afford to let go, but she was also truly ready to let go. She rediscovered lost passions, rebuilt connections with friends that shared her interests, and arranged to volunteer at her former workplace to keep the connection with her inner purpose. Her plans and new possibilities ignited an energy and vitality she had long forgotten. Retirement planning shifted from a year away to months. Confident and secure, she stepped into her retirement, her rebirth, ready to be MORE.

For many people, retirement is the time to finally embrace life's passions and purpose. Retirement is not an end; it is a new beginning. Once you allow yourself to explore your desires, as Tricia did, life can become even richer and more fulfilling. My spouse's retirement and the flexibility of my work are allowing us to embrace our "gypsy phase." We want to live closer to our families, but in climates that support our health and vitality. The exploration continues, feeding our passion to thrive and our purpose to create quality family time.

Meaning through Loss

Finding and maintaining belonging, exploring and living your passions, following and fulfilling your purpose, will move you forward. These essential MORE elements expand your possibilities to live life fully and create natural abundance and success in your life. Living MORE will not exclude you from experiencing life's extreme challenges. It will, however, support you in how you process, learn, and live with them. Job loss, retirement, a death of a loved one, and catastrophic events such as fires, hurricanes, and floods all challenge meaning in our lives.

We live in a small place—a connected community and safe place where news, especially bad news, travels fast. Recently, news of the murder of a young man has shaken all of us to our core. His life had been fraught with challenge, both physical and mental. A client of mine had worked with him for years, connecting him to people who could help him learn healthy work and life skills. She had held fundraisers to build the finances needed for surgery he required. Heartstruck, she and I tried to process his death. While understanding the motives of those who ended his life is beyond both of us, we do know that there are ways to make meaning of his life, to use his struggle and determination to inspire and lead others. The grief is new, the pain persistent, but we know that actions can be taken to ensure his life will not be forgotten. This gives us hope, comfort, and meaning.

Just when we least expect it, life continually brings forth challenges to stretch us. My husband is one such person. Alan was diagnosed with an extremely rare cancer, aggressive T-cell lymphoma, just as his professional trajectory was at an all-time high. He was considered one of the college's most outstanding professors. Students loved his courses, and colleagues sought out his mentorship and counsel. As the name implies, the cancer happened suddenly and aggressively. Alan and I were preparing a group of select students for an immersion semester with us in the Caribbean, on the small island of Carriacou. All plans came to a screeching halt. Life as we knew it was on hold and then changed forever.

Our time now centered around hospitals, doctors, nurses, medications, bacteria, and the ups and downs of chemotherapy. We had an amazing support group of family and friends. Former students, whom we affectionately came to call our younglings, were frequent visitors. Making meaning of this experience was important for both of us to move past the frozen state of "why?" As lifetime educators, we chose to learn from our experiences and teach what the cancer journey taught us, in order to support and ease the cancer journey for others.

After a quick remission and favorable first round of chemotherapy, we were devastated to learn of the cancer's quick return. An allogeneic bone marrow transplant (BMT) requiring donor stem cells was the only option—a procedure that was not possible in our hometown. Flights to New York City became the norm as Alan was repeatedly prepped, prodded, tested, and examined. He had a strong negative reaction to a trial drug that he had agreed to take in preparation for the BMT. Many thought we had lost him at that point, as he spent fourteen days in ICU, his skin stretched almost past recognition by the fluids that the doctors used in an attempt to flush his system. Surviving that abuse, Alan received further chemotherapy and full-body radiation, taking him within a whisper of death. We were blessed that both his brother and sister were a 100 percent blood match and willing to do whatever was needed. Replacing Alan's stem cells with his brother's, the doctors masterfully manipulated another trial of countless drugs over the course of many months, allowing Alan's body to accept and own his new bone marrow and blood cells.

Throughout this extensive, excruciating, painful, and exhausting ordeal, Alan knew he would survive. He had more to do, more to teach, and more to learn. It was not a "positive attitude"; it was his belief—a knowing in every cell of his body that he would live beyond his cancer. He never picked up the end of the cancer tug-of-war rope and fought cancer; he just allowed the cancer to pass through his body and be replaced by stronger, healthier cells needed to rebuild. Living through and beyond cancer has become part of the meaning in his life.

While extreme health challenges stretch our ability to create meaning in our lives, the void of death can rob us of our ability to move toward any sense of meaning or purpose.

Colleen, a client of mine, lost all of her children in a tragic accident many years ago. She was devastated—mentally, physically, and spiritually torn to pieces. Moving far away, seeking escape, solace, and belonging in a warm tropical location, over time she developed a need and desire to understand death. It became a mission and purpose for Colleen as she studied the work of researchers, including Elizabeth Kübler-Ross. Her studies led her to write a series of stories told from the perspective of her children's angels, to help other young people understand death. Through the stories, she made meaning of her loss, an avenue for her children to live on, and a positive impact on the lives of others.

Making meaning from the death of a loved one evolves in its own time and process. It does not mean that you have to write a book, establish a foundation, or sit on the board of a charity. What it does mean is that it is okay to feel and internalize the loss, understanding that your loss will always be a companion. When my father died, I felt a fissure created in my soul, a hole that can never be filled. Healing merely stitches together the fissure's ragged edges. We do not "get over"; we only need to move on, to move forward. Creating meaning allows us to honor and internalize the best of the people we have lost, carrying their energy forever forward in a new combination that enables us to live fully MORE.

The impact of loss on our psyche and spirit is amplified when we find ourselves within a catastrophic disaster, loss on a mass scale. I have friends who escaped from the horror and ongoing terror of war in Bosnia and the Sudan. Loss of their homes, families, and all that was normal impassioned them to embrace every step in their struggle to succeed, to create meaning from all that they had endured. They found belonging within small communities in Vermont and purpose through new opportunities. They learned English, navigated a new culture, achieved college degrees, fostered friendships, raised their families, and now thrive within new careers.

Most of us cannot begin to understanding of that kind of struggle, living within the fear and uncertainty of a war zone. Yet, fear and uncertainty are no strangers to those of us who have been impacted by the devastation of a nature disaster, when Mother Nature changes the rules by which we live and dismantles our lives.

At three a.m. the morning of October 9, 2017, my husband and I were two of thousands of people evacuated from Santa Rosa, California, as the unprecedented massive wildfires leaped roadways and engulfed entire neighborhoods and the surrounding hillsides. In the dark, toxic smoke-filled apartment, we threw a few things into bags and drove through the eerie unlit streets, searching for a path forward. We sat in shock for hours in a large parking lot with hundreds of other people, watching the dense smoke from the fires as they swallowed homes, schools, and businesses. Realizing that staying where we were was not an option, we chose a path forward, seeking safety and support.

Just as when our friends and family, only a month before, had their lives, homes, and country obliterated by Hurricanes Irma and Maria, trauma became our new norm. Living in the United States, we were fortunate to be able to drive to safety, to seek and receive the support of strangers, our insurance company, and FEMA. Not so for people in the islands, trapped in the rubble of what was left of their homes; there was no escape. Roads impassable, no power, no water, almost no way forward. The only choice was to work together, support each other, and seek ways to survive.

No matter how hard and how traumatizing it is, moving forward is the only direction. The process is painfully slow and exceedingly challenging. Recovery is a long and arduous process; it breeds equal measures of fear, frustration, and mistrust with unparalleled humanity, creativity, and commitment. The Chinese word for crisis is a combination of two characters, the first *danger,* the second, *opportunity.*

Crisis, devastation, or loss is always an opportunity to move forward, to create meaning and purpose as we build and strengthen our common bonds.

Meaning and MORE

Creating meaning in your life requires you to take action, make decisions, and choose your course. Meaning requires you to move beyond the role of victim and step into the role of the empowered. Living within your comfort zone or status quo stagnates your ability to embrace meaning and MORE in your life. MORE allows you to move beyond the human-virus state. Your meaning evolves the more you value and engage in your journey. Meaning becomes your guide, your muse, and your compass.

You make time to create calm, reflective, quiet spaces and moments in your life. You actively seek out places and people with which to belong and let go of those that limit and deplete you. Living your meaning opens you to new opportunities and acquaintances that will further the evolution of your potential. Creating meaning requires you to own your potential, foster and develop positive relationships, and understand when your emotions are blocking you from moving forward.

Meaning brings support and comfort in your darkest hours, transforming challenges and losses into insights for learning and growth. You embrace challenges, setbacks, and crises as opportunities to make meaning and enrich your purpose. MORE's core element of meaning provides you with resiliency, a knowing that no matter what transpires, you have the capacity to use it to move forward. As you live your meaning, you expand your ability for compassion, spreading kindness in the darkest of corners, supporting meaning-making and the potential for yourself and others. The process evolves over time. As you focus inward and reflect on your sense of belonging, reconnect with your passions, explore ways to fulfill your purpose, and use loss as an opportunity for growth, you create meaning. It is not a passive activity; it requires choices, actions, and *owning* your worth.

Owning

Meaning

Relationships

Emotions

beliefs & baggage
control
perceptions
failures
health & vitality
spirit
optimism
worth

Blog Post: Mirror, Mirror

"Mirror, Mirror, on the wall, who's the fairest of them all?" cackles the demanding wicked queen. My sisters and I sit transfixed in front of the large black-and-white screen of our cabinet television as we watch the unfolding of Walt Disney's tale of *Snow White and the Seven Dwarfs*.

There is something about the honesty of the mirror—the fact that the mirror always sees things that the queen cannot—that makes me ponder about what I "see" in my own mirror. Like the wicked queen in *Snow White,* many of us are "mirror challenged." It is hard for us to see ourselves and our circumstances from any other perspective than the one we tell ourselves to see. We are what we believe. We see what we expect to see. We see what we choose to see. Our perspective is unique to us.

It's not until we step into the changing room of owning that we are forced to see ourselves from multiple perspectives. Naked in the glaring lights and three-way mirror, we have an opportunity to see ourselves from a new perspective. Not a condemning, fault-finding perspective, but an honest, deep look at all of our strengths and blessings. Accepting our faults, those things we have been avoiding or denying, allows us to create new opportunities of learning and creating MORE.

So the first phase of moving forward is to *look* deeply into the mirrors of our lives. Look clearly, honestly, and emphatically at all that consumes your life. Without judgment, excuses, or "yeah, buts"—just look. Take note, make a list, categorize it, color it, code it—whatever works to make it as complete as you can. Then *own* it. Owning is the second key element of living MORE. Owning allows you to embrace, increase, rewrite, or release any aspect that is limiting your potential.

Owning

MORE's core element of owning acknowledges that each of us is responsible for our health, perceptions, and beliefs. Owning requires MORE individuals to consciously turn failure into opportunities for learning, for creating, and for meaning-making. Owning is about choice; it requires persistence and a strong dose of optimism. MORE individuals own and live their worth, continually seeking to expand their potential.

MORE's second core component of owning is centered on our individual and collective needs to achieve, succeed, and grow. The human virus state of our "always-on" culture not only prevents us from connecting and creating owning in our lives, but also traps us in a fear-based victim state in which life and events happen to us, like the headlights of an oncoming car in the eyes of a deer, paralyzing us from moving forward. We blame; we complain; we ridicule, breeding negativity within our bodies, lives, and workplace. We substitute food for feelings, sarcasm for humor, pessimism for possibilities, and blame for opportunity.

I know I lived through my years of victimhood and blame, plagued by low self-esteem and self-worth, for much of my teens and twenties. I used cutting sarcasm as humor and would brush it off by saying, "I was just kidding. Can't you take a joke?" At a deep level, I meant it. I subconsciously used sarcasm to level the playing field, putting others down to build myself up. I went through a lot of counseling, courses, reflections, and readings before I could look in the mirror and honestly acknowledge this in myself. The acknowledgment meant I could no longer blame others or my circumstances for how I felt about myself. I had to move beyond victimhood and fault-finding, toward ownership and acceptance. These were my first steps toward understanding and owning my worth.

Owning Our Beliefs and Baggage

We are all born with a subconscious set of luggage. Every experience and interaction is put in that luggage. The older we get, the more luggage we acquire. We continually tote around the good, the bad, and the ugly of our lives. Being that our brains focus first on the negative and negate the positive, we lug around a larger collection of what's wrong, awful, and hurtful about our lives and ourselves. Our always-on, multitasking lives add exponentially to the psychic weight of our luggage, keeping us in a constant state of never finished, never enough, and never perfect.

This weight creates the numbness of the human virus state. Our ability to raise awareness, clarity, and harmony in our lives is packed deep within our mountain of mental luggage. We mask our need for harmony by creating addictions mentally, physically, or spiritually. Mental addictions transform into anger, anxiety, and depression. We become myopic in our awareness of self and others. The problems are always out there, not within us. Physical addictions lead us to become obsessive in how we eat, drink, and treat our bodies. We use food to feed our emotions and problems, not to nourish our bodies and cells. Even exercise can become an addiction, as we look to control and create an extreme form of ourselves. Spiritual addictions use spiritual practices as escapes from owning our responsibilities and as walls to hide behind, taking us outside of our current realities and negatively impacting our relationships.

Numbness and addiction do not happen to just a few other people—they happen to all of us. I moved through phases of medicating my lack of self-worth with food and alcohol, only to shift those addictions into addictions to exercise and diets. In my compulsive lifestyles, I continually sought "outside-in" validation and comfort. I wanted others to validate my talents, my abilities, my looks, my worth—to validate me.

Once I recognized that I needed to own my choices physically, mentally, and spiritually, I learned to shift my focus inward, reflect and connect with exercise, and use meditation/prayer that supported who I was meant to become. I consciously and methodically unpacked my mental baggage, the thoughts and beliefs I had been carrying for years. Just when I thought I had it all figured out, when I had mastered Owning, life changes made me realize that Owning is an ongoing process of life.

Learning to own and live your worth is a common theme in my coaching. No matter how outwardly successful someone appears to others, within the confidentiality of the coaching conversations, the person's limited sense of worth will surface.

> Vanessa was one such client. I had known her many years before my coaching career. She had shared with me the horrors and abuse of her childhood and first marriage. I knew the heavy emotional baggage she carried, and I was surprised when she reached out to me for coaching. "Vanessa, you know my coaching is not about digging deep into your emotional issues and past," I responded. "Coaching is about acknowledging the past as the past, clarifying how you can use it for learning, and creating opportunities to move forward. You may want to seek out a psychologist who can assist you in processing your past in more depth."

> Vanessa was confident that she was ready to move beyond her past barriers and begin coaching. While many sessions involved her regressing into "I just need you to know this," she learned to stretch her thinking, view past events from a new perspective, gain fresh insights, and create small actions to move forward. Vanessa stumbled forward, and she stumbled back. She

postponed sessions and then seemingly disappeared from contact, even though we had one final session together. Months passed. Finally, she reconnected and asked to schedule her final coaching session. She had moved into a healthy environment and found work where she was respected. I was in awe as we compared her current life, thoughts, and behaviors to those she had when she began her coaching journey. It was not until she shared her current situation with me that she became consciously aware of how much she had grown and evolved. Vanessa had learned to own her worth and take control of her life.

Owning your beliefs and baggage does not mean you have to always carry them with you. The owning requires you to recognize that baggage is weighing you down and limiting your ability to move forward and evolve. The baggage can be both mental and physical. Begin with your closets and cupboards. Sell, give away, gift; let others gain from your release. The physical process can often trigger the inner baggage release. Own your freedom from the weight of the past.

Owning and Control

The toxic multilayering of our lives can also leave us overwhelmed, depressed, and exhausted. Our life and our experiences seem out of our control. We are helpless riders on a manic merry-go-round. The endless spinning throws us off balance, making it impossible to focus on how to own and control our lives. Many individuals have sought me out as a coach because of the lack of control they feel within their personal and professional lives. They are victims; life happens to them, not for them. Trapped on their endless merry-go-round, they fear staying on as much as stopping. Staying on the merry-go-round continues the vicious cycle. Stopping seems impossible; it might cause their world to "fly off," scattering randomly in unmanageable fragments, impossible to reconstruct.

> Tyra used that exact metaphor as she described her professional life and the negative impact it was having on her personal life and her true-life passion. Through coaching, she began to consider the possibility of pausing the merry-go-round. She began to reflect on ways she could shift her perspective, her actions, and her reactions to open new opportunities for moving forward. The key for Tyra to regain control was to say no, which was a challenge for her. She tied her sense of self and worth to always being the person who could, and would, do everything. Saying no meant she had to recognize that doing and worth are the same. Doing gave her an extrinsic and shallow sense of worth. Learning to say no meant that she had to seek, recognize, and foster her intrinsic worth. With practice, "no" became empowering and allowed her to move her journey forward by owning her responsibility to herself, her passion, and her meaning. Her MORE core elements of meaning and owning intertwined, supporting her evolution.

As your personal and professional merry-go-round slows to a stop, your vision clears. Events, relationships, and experiences become separate entities, not a never-ending, spinning blur of vertigo. Vision creates clarity, clarity leads to owning options, options open to choice, and choosing allows you to create MORE.

Owning and Perceptions

No one sees the world, events, or situations the same way you do. No one else knows what you think unless you tell the person.

Relationships do not come with mind-reading capabilities. Have you ever heard or caught yourself saying any of the following? "If you really cared, you'd know." "I shouldn't have to tell you." "I already told you."

Owning your perceptions means you acknowledge that communication is a complex interaction between two or more people. The complexity results from the fact that your perception is unique to you; no one else experiences the world as you do. You see the world through your unique lenses and filters, and if you desire others to hear, recognize, and understand you, you need to communicate with patience and persistence.

Staying aware and continually, consciously communicating is difficult in any relationship. The longer the relationship and the more time we spend together, the more challenging it is to stay aware of our assumptions and perceptions.

> Dennis, a young entrepreneur, is in business with a few of his family members. He is the one who takes the lead on all things and is the first to speak up for the entire team. He processes the world orally and hence is always talking. The others process the world internally; they think before they speak and often are unsure of just how to phrase what they actually want to say. In one of our private coaching conversations, I asked Dennis how the others felt about his vision and new ideas for the business. There was silence. He did not know what the others would say and had never thought to ask them. He took their silence as acceptance, not realizing that they never had enough time to process all that he shared. The insight challenged him to step back, begin to ask questions, allow time for thought and reflection, and then make time to truly listen.

Truly listening meant he had to move beyond his preconceived ideas of why and how the others did what they did. Dennis realized that he could not continue to see them through the lens of their past selves, who he "knows" them to be. His lenses were preventing him from seeing the growth they were making personally and professionally. Becoming aware of his conditioned assumptions allowed Dennis to monitor his assumptions and begin to release them. Communication became a two-way conversation, one that honored the needs of everyone. Owning allowed Dennis to foster his relationships and create MORE.

Most of us have experienced this in one relationship or another. It happens a lot with our parents. You may have experienced your mother treating you the same way she did when you were a child, not acknowledging that you are an adult, have been to college or learned a trade, and have a job or a family of your own. While you cannot change your mother's perception, you can change your responses to her. Knowing and accepting that she sees you from the past and for whatever reasons is unable to see you as an adult in the present allows you to let go of your negative responses. Letting go allows you to move forward. Your mother can be who she is and you to be who you are. I was well into my thirties before my grandmother and I agreed that we could disagree and still love each other. It did not mean she stopped trying to control me, but I learned to let her controlling statements pass through me without hitting my negative response trigger.

Owning Our Failures

Many people seek to avoid failure at any cost. They see failure as a sign of weakness and worthlessness. Avoiding failure means that you limit your abilities to grow or try anything new. My perfectionist tendencies blocked my growth for years. Perfectionism kept me from trying anything at which I could not immediately excel or do perfectly. Learning and accepting that perfection is in the moment, this moment, with all of now's imperfections, was a challenge for me. It still can take a conscious effort on my part to make that shift, but the shift is freeing and always opens the door for moving forward.

One of my big perfection challenges came when I decided to learn aikido. I had taken a personal development workshop taught through the Filipino martial art of *arnis* (knife fighting). While our "knives" were rubber bicycle handles, I had never been part of a more intense program connecting one's mind, body, and spirit. The experience left me with a desire to learn a martial art.

Based on the general explanations I had heard during the workshop, I decided that tai chi might be too "soft" a martial art and karate too "hard." In my mind, with no real research (this was pre-personal computers and internet searches), I decided the perfect martial art for me was aikido. I sought out an aikido dojo, called the sensei, registered at his home, and went to the next class. My perfectionism button went into alarm mode as I observed the students, of all ages and sizes, dive-rolling over each other's backs and stacks of backs. *Ahhhhh!* my brain screamed. *This is gymnastics!*

I had to push past my natural desire to be perfect and learn to embrace the opportunities that come from imperfection and learning. My aikido partner was gracious enough to meet me two mornings a week so that we could practice our moves and techniques. Pushing past perfection, learning from my mistakes, and forcing myself to put in the extra effort allowed me to develop the skills and abilities to pass my first level. "Perfect," I learned, is in the moment. It is embracing where you are right now and knowing that from this "perfect" place and time, you have the ability to own your way forward.

Not owning failure requires you to create excuses and find scapegoats. I did just that after my divorce and after being fired from a job. It took time and a lot of self-reflection and humility to own my role in each situation. The owning is where my turning points happened. Owning allowed me to let go, learn, and grow. New opportunities and directions became possible that before had been invisible to me.

Owning your failure means that you use your failure as a learning opportunity rather than another link in the "I'm not worthy, I'm no good, I'm so stupid" ball and chain that you drag behind your low self-worth. I work with coaching clients who are developing their ability to own their failures. They are beginning their owning by paying attention to how they think and speak of their failures. Whenever they hear or catch themselves thinking that they have failed at something, they consciously tell themselves, "This is a learning opportunity." That statement allows them to shift their perspective and open their minds to create new insights and ideas. Interestingly enough, all truly successful people, including Bill Gates, Oprah Winfrey, Henry Ford, and J. K. Rowling, saw their mistakes and failures as opportunities for learning, adapting, revising, and growing.

Owning Our Health and Vitality

No matter our position, age, or interests, we all need to make time to manage our health—mentally, physically, and spiritually. MORE requires that we take ownership of our choices to eat healthily, get enough sleep, and exercise in ways that promote our sense of vitality. MORE supports a life of harmony through the integration of our professional and personal lives. MORE recognizes the importance and benefits of owning our connection to spirit within and around us. How we incorporate, practice, and embody our health mentally, physically, and spiritually is a choice. MORE requires us to increase our self-awareness and make conscious decisions that maximize our potential, purpose, and feelings of worth and well-being.

Like many of you, I continue to be challenged with finding harmony in my health, vitality, and the stuff of life. I used to believe that there was one perfect combination and magic balance that one could attain, maintain, and "Ta-da," achieve health and vitality for life. Just when I thought I had it mastered, life would happen. Something new added to my mix: a new location, a new job, a new position, or a new relationship. Life events, things that were beyond my control like my husband's cancer and my father's death, played havoc with my ability to maintain harmony in my health, vitality, and life.

All the new, out-of-my-control events increased my stress levels, played havoc on my sleep, and limited my ability to make healthy choices. It is at those times when healthy choices are essential. I forced myself to turn off the television, shut down the Internet, and pull away from social media. Those simple steps alone allowed me to create the time I needed to move toward health and vitality again. I continually work to develop my abilities to reduce stress through guided meditation programs and simple daily exercise like morning stretches and going for a walk. I make a grocery list before shopping and take the time to create simple, healthy meals for my husband and myself. Walks and meals together give both of us downtime to replenish. We actively seek out support and guidance from a range of health care providers to ensure we are acknowledging and paying attention to our full health spectrum. Together, we keep each other motivated to own our health. Many of my clients have created other motivators for moving. They take yoga classes, join a gym, or make concerted efforts to walk the dog each day. These activities positively impact your health and vitality.

The aging process can bring its own set of challenges to our established patterns of health and vitality within our bodies and our minds. If we say we are "over the hill" and "too old," we are resigning ourselves to societal and cultural beliefs about what comes with growing older. The closer you examine your thoughts and beliefs about aging, the greater the opportunities you can create for owning health and vitality throughout your life. Living to thrive, not surviving to die. Owning your aging means you embrace your wisdom years by surrounding yourself with people who make you happy, create activities that promote your health, and live your life to its fullest. Like with other owning opportunities, we can shift our perspective on aging and open new avenues for embracing our growing wisdom.

Catherine was famous for saying she just had no energy for cooking or exercising, two things she used to love doing. Her work was all-consuming, draining her time and her energy. On deeper examination of her schedule and priorities, Catherine found that she could adjust her morning routine a few days a week to include exercise, which gradually became a natural part of her day. Not satisfied with her routine, Catherine bumped up her level and commitment by booking one-on-one yoga lessons at her home. When she was comfortable with her yoga skills, she further extended herself and joined an early morning class twice a week.

Her love of cooking returned by booking stay-at-home dates with her husband. Together, they would immerse in the cooking process, exploring new recipes and indulging in new tastes and flavors they created. Catherine and her husband cherished the time spent in conversation and thrived in their joint creative process.

By committing herself to schedule specific times and days for her exercise and cooking with her husband,

Catherine realized that she was placing her life and her needs on the same level as everything she scheduled for work. She deserved the time, and owning the time allowed her to honor her health and vitality.

One of my biggest teachers in owning health and vitality was my father. Although he had MS for more than half of his eighty-three years, he pushed himself beyond every new physical limitation. Over the years, he progressed from walking with a cane to walking with a walker to driving a scooter and finally a motorized wheelchair. He went on experimental drug programs and tried a variety of natural and homeopathic therapies. No matter the limitations, he continued to pursue his passions of photography, music, and woodworking. Thanks to the constant support of my mother, they kept traveling the world, creating new adventures and countless memories.

While there is no magical balance in life or perfect combination of activities, there is a never-ending opportunity to learn, explore, try, adapt, and blend owning your health and vitality.

Owning and Spirit

Owning your spiritual connection can expand the depth of MORE in your life. Spirituality may take the form of organized religion for some and a more flexible view of the world and our connections to spirit for others.

A number of my clients truly own their faith, their church, and religion. In turn, their church and religion support who they are and open possibilities for greater growth and acceptance of others.

Having moved recently, Mickey took some time to find the church community that supported her spiritual needs. She quickly moved away from the communities that demonstrated judgment and condemnation of difference. Owning what she believed she needed and desired from a church community led her to one she could call home. She knew she had found the right spiritual community when the service, and conversations following service, lifted her spirit and filled her heart with joy.

I have also had clients who added a quiet, meditative time into their day, some for just a minute or two; others make a morning ritual that includes time on their own to think, reflect, meditate, or write.

Joella was controlled by her anxieties, living her life in an overwhelmed state. She felt trapped and defeated. Her life began to shift as she added meditative moments into her day. Joella discovered that by staying aware of her feelings and triggers, she could pause, breathe, and quiet her mind. She noted that the more she practiced using her mini-meditations, the more her sense of anxiety and stress diminished. The more tranquil her mind, the more space she had to connect with her inner spirit. Her inner spirit brought happiness and joy back into her life, and she referred to herself as "effervescent."

Richard had become disillusioned with his church and what he viewed as the hypocrisy of many members of the congregation. He stopped attending but missed his connection with his spiritual practice. Richard began exploring what exactly was missing. He was surprised to discover that he felt the greatest connection to his spiritual self while he was walking his dog. It was the alone time, in nature, with his unconditionally-loving dog that allowed him to go within and connect with his spiritual self. Owning the walks as his spiritual practice fed his soul and centered his thoughts. Reconnecting and trusting his spirit allowed him to release negative and nagging feelings and open up positive ideas for moving forward.

Some of my most powerful connections to spirit have come in the vastness of the outdoors. One of my spiritual places is the Canadian Rockies. When I pause at an opening on a mountain trail to drink in the majesty and immenseness of the rugged peaks and the power of the tectonic plates that created them, I feel insignificant to the larger picture. As diminutive as I feel, if I pay attention, breathe in the clean, crisp air, and exhale into the space, I realize I am one with all around me. The splendor of the mountains, the magnificence of spirit, is within me and surrounds me.

Another special spiritual place for me is in the Caribbean. My first trip to the Caribbean was aboard a three-masted tall ship. The widow's net is an assembly of lines that hang from the bowsprit of the ship. At night, I would take a couple of floating mats, lay them over the ropes, and sleep suspended between the merged blackness of the sea and sky. Stars twinkled above, while moonlight danced in sparkles on the lapping waves. It was a transformative experience. I was connected, one with the sea, the stars, the universe.

Owning your spiritual core requires that you make time to go within and explore your thoughts, beliefs, and connection to a large purpose. Genuine spiritual connection feeds your life, expands possibilities, and leads the way forward. It fosters your need to be and share love, kindness, and peace. Spirit connects us all; owning our spirit allows us to own our connection to each other and the planet.

Owning and Optimism

Owning requires us to look at our lives and situations from the broad, open perspective of the eagle rather than the minute, narrow viewpoint of a field mouse. It demands that we move beyond the details and excuses that limit us and seek new pathways and opportunities for becoming more of who we are meant to be. It requires us to make time to pause and expand our outlook. We may not all be natural optimists, but individuals living MORE know that optimism can be practiced, fostered, and learned. MORE individuals know that we are holistic beings—minds, thoughts, and beliefs play out in our physiology and psychology. Negative thoughts create ill ease and even dis-ease in our lives.

Simple words can trap us in the negative. Words like *should, but, can't,* and *never* limit your ability to move forward. They form mental roadblocks that stop and derail insights and new opportunities. They make you wrong before you can even have a chance to try. I was a master at using these words and limiting my potential. They kept me safe, risk-free, and stagnated. I would criticize my efforts with *should haves,* discounting and making the things I had done wrong. *Yes, but* always negated the insights and ideas others were sharing with me, making them incorrect and my excuse right. I closed the door to new possibilities with *I can't* and limited my ability to expand my potential with *I never.* When I recognized the need to reword my thoughts and automatic responses in conversations, I was amazed at how often I used those words. Each negative word I acknowledged allowed me to reword my thoughts and statements, and over time, I began eliminating them from my conscious and unconscious vocabulary. I became more optimistic, open, and creative. I began to take risks and do things I had only imagined. I went skydiving, I traveled internationally, I moved to the Caribbean, I moved to the United States, I began my own business, and the list continues.

What unique opportunities will open up for you when you remove the negatives from your vocabulary?

> Brittany got pregnant at a very young age, married the father of her child, and lived in misery and depression. She was a talented, gifted businesswoman who felt trapped by her life circumstance; she believed there was no other path, no other option. Through her coaching process, Brittany began to recognize that she did have choices. She realized that should have, can't, and if only were merely words, not her reality. Brittany developed strategies for creating change. She and her spouse went to counseling. Shifting her limiting thoughts and comments from despair and pessimism to see things with hope and optimism, over time she realized she needed to end the marriage. Staying married kept her life stagnant and her future limited. Divorce meant walking through messy, emotional reactions from her husband, but she knew it was the only path forward. Divorce now in process, Brittany still seeks to foster a conscious and constructive co-parenting relationship that provides the best for their son. Brittany now owns her optimism and sees herself and her future as vibrant, exciting, and full of possibilities.

Owning Your Worth

The ever-changing economic landscape may have you dealing with a long series of setbacks. Devalued and disrespected, you can feel battered and abused by forces outside your control. You may be one of the people forced out of a longtime career or whose job description morphed into roles well beyond your expertise and interest. As you become wedged into a constant threat state, your overall health and well-being are burdened and broken down by fear, hopelessness, criticism, and marginalization.

Feeling valued is central to our sense of worth. The more you seek outside validation, the less you get, and there is the catch. Value does not come from outside. It comes from within, from who you are and who you desire to become. If you do not appreciate your worth, no one else will. Ironically, even if others do value you, if you do not believe it, you will not see it.

You may have learned that if you value yourself, you are conceited and self-serving. Value is not vanity. Value is synonymous with self-worth. We all know people who continually downplay their importance, their abilities, and their value to others. They are impossible to compliment, always putting down what they have done. If you live or work with such a person, you may have even stopped thanking him or her for things.

Not owning your value and your worth keeps you in a victim state. When you are the victim, outside forces control who you are and how you perceive yourself and your possibilities. You become a doormat, allowing the actions and beliefs of others to trample your worth. Trodden and abused, you feel marginalized and constricted within. Owning your worth and living MORE requires you to stand up, brush yourself off, and look in the mirror. See the person you are meant to be and open yourself to the concept that you deserve to be MORE.

Change like this does not happen overnight. You have spent years listening to self-talk that has limited you, perhaps caring too much about what others think or buying into the limiting beliefs taught by your friends and family. If you have ever tried to change a habit, whether it is biting your nails or losing weight, you know it takes time. There are no quick fixes. In your journey toward MORE, you will begin to realize that your limiting habits are multilayered and weblike. But by identifying and starting with changing just one small action, you will start to reveal other opportunities for opening new directions and possibilities. Your mind only knows what you tell it. Time to tell it a new story, the story about you and your potential. The way forward begins with one small positive thought at a time. Patience and persistence become your best allies.

I know this drill all too well. I've been there myself, but life and a whole lot of valuable "teachers" have taught me to question my excuses, move beyond closed doors, and seek numerous other avenues to living life fully and expanding my potential. It's not the easy path; it takes daring, commitment, and trust. My journey continues, as does yours.

Owning Our Lives

Owning allows us to embrace life's changes and challenges, accept them, and continually reinvent to move with them. Whether the life change is marriage, divorce, childbirth, elder care, career transition, menopause, or man-opause—"life happens." We create MORE by owning our choices in embracing and creating the best of whom we choose to be within the darkest valleys and brightest peaks of life.

risk
magic
giving & receiving
motivation
listening
culture
letting go

Relationships

Meaning

Owning

Emotions

Blog Post: Tricycles and Training Wheels

Do you remember that butterflies-in-your-stomach feeling of excitement you get when you are trying something new, like the first time your dad let go of your bike and you wobbled down the road on your own? You progressed from the three-wheeled support of your tricycle, which you had learned to pedal at manic speed, to the shaky security of training wheels and now to the freedom of two wheels and new horizons. You were invincible. Surely, one of your parents was close by if needed, but you were free, on your own, no support necessary.

Growing up is like that. Parents support their children to the best of their abilities. Teachers guide and coach their students to embrace and expand their learning. Friends encourage or challenge us to try new things and seek out new adventures. When we are children, there is always (hopefully) someone there to support us, guide us, and pick us up when we fall and get hurt. Then we become big boys and girls, young adults, and we are on our own: no supports, no training wheels. Just life and us. Freedom.

Most of the time, we are comfortable with that independence. That is, until life happens: job loss, relationship failure, financial challenge, health crisis, aging parents, or death. If you are like me, it is times like these when it would be nice to have a little support, a bit of guidance, and a touch of comfort. At these times, life reminds us that we are not in this alone. We need each other. We need the support of our family, friends, and neighbors.

If this has not happened to you yet, it will. Life is like that. Of course, we can choose to stay closed, isolated, and independent, "me-focused." The isolation creates an illusion of control and protection, but ironically, it just barricades us from belonging, support, and compassion.

Those of us who have been fortunate enough to be parents or teachers know that along with the young ones' pride in their accomplishments is the even greater gratification of giving and championing the growth and needs of others. We are in this life together; no one enters this world alone, and, as my father's hospice nurse said, "No one should leave this world alone."

MORE relationships form the training wheels needed to support our journeys.

Relationships

MORE relationships are founded on honesty, respect, and acceptance for others and ourselves. Your relationship with yourself and your perception of your worth and potential influence your relationships with others. Every MORE relationship recognizes that caring and compassionate relationships do not magically happen; they are a continuous work in progress as we each change and evolve into who we are meant to be. MORE individuals recognize that their personal evolution and journey intertwines their lives with a great variety of relationships. Some evolve along with us; others provide us with passing opportunities for us to learn and grow.

Relationships and Risk

MORE relationships are risky; they require us to stretch, be open, and be vulnerable. Risk demands that we share our feelings, knowing that it is not necessarily how others feel. We risk being shut down or misunderstood, which compels us to persist in sharing and clarifying our thoughts and our needs. Risking can put you off balance, trigger nervousness, and make you feel uncomfortable. It is within this disequilibrium that relationships gain clarity. The clarity will allow you to either strengthen and further the relationship or recognize the limitations and finality of the relationship. Either way, you have opportunities to learn and grow into who you are meant to be, your MORE.

> Nahome is an extremely successful and respected professional. She is actively engaged in her community and prides herself on her service to others. From the outside, no one would suspect that she was inwardly terrified of never finding a husband. She questions the motivations of men she meets and fears that she will just be hurt again. Her need to complete herself

through a relationship is so intense that she finds herself settling for the first guy who comes along. He flatters her, gives her expensive gifts, and takes her on impressive outings, but he always fails to meet her expectations, her unwritten rules for relationships. In our coaching conversations, Nahome recognizes her pattern, yet cannot give up on her "relationship rules." She is not ready to risk believing that her best relationships will come from creating a loving, positive foundational relationship with herself. She equates loving herself with being lonely and living a life of emptiness. Her door to creating a loving, fulfilling relationship remains shut.

A positive relationship with yourself begins with your sense of self-worth. Belief in your worth can open or block positive relationships in our lives.

Jake desires a love relationship that makes him feel complete, yet his experience and low sense of self-worth have prevented him from even asking a woman out on a date. He saw dating as the only avenue to finding his perfect mate. Through the coaching process, Jake stepped away from his fear of dating and began to create actions that supported him in building his self-confidence. He made time to take part in new interests and activities, allowing him to develop a wider variety of friends. Jake tried things he had never made time for but always wanted to do, exploring new places and creating new friends. The more he risked and opened himself to new experiences and meeting new people, the more his sense of self-worth expanded. Jake's overall energy shifted from dark and closed to open and energetic. Women became drawn to his positive energy and the potential. Jake sees now that establishing an intimate relationship is only a matter of time, patience, and risk. He knows that taking a risk to begin a conversation, to ask a woman out, and to open himself up to vulnerability is his avenue to love.

Many of us get in the way of creating positive relationships by focusing only on the other person. We concentrate on our list of "must haves," what we believe we want based on superficial and unrealistic ideals.

Doug just wants to find the perfect woman to marry. He has a very clear list of who she needs to be and how she needs to look. When I asked him, "What list of qualities will the woman you are looking for have for her perfect mate?" he paused. A long pause. He had never thought about a love relationship from the partner's perspective. It was the first time he had considered what he was bringing to a partnership. Seeing a love relationship through the eyes of the other made Doug realize that a real relationship was going to require him to risk. The perfect mate was more than just a checklist of qualities; she would require him to be open, willing to communicate and share his feelings and to work through challenges. The vulnerability of the idea unnerved him: "That scares me." Stepping up to his fear, Doug began to see dating as an avenue for getting to know another person through opening up about himself. Dates were no longer a one-sided "perfect mate" interview.

Without risk, you will limit your relationships. Without risk, you cannot be truly heard. Without risk, you will limit love. Without risk, you will minimize your ability to grow into your potential.

Relationships and Magic

Sunday nights growing up were all about *The Wonderful World of Disney*. My sisters and I were allowed to eat our dinner in the living room as we watched the Disney magic unfold. Whether the episode involved families, friends, or couples, their issues were always resolved by the end of the hour. Love happened magically, and of course, all ended happily ever after. Now we know realistically that those were stories, fantasy, and fiction; yet, many of us will still hold the people closest to us to those same standards. Even when we have grown up with families that are codependent, dysfunctional, and argumentative, we still seem to think that the Disney ideal is real. If only we could meet the right person, look a certain way, or have the people closest to us change their behaviors.

When you focus on relationships from the outside; wanting others to tell you that you are amazing, bright, beautiful, and creative, you fail to realize that the words of appreciation and acknowledgment need to first come from within yourself. You only see and hear what you believe. Belief comes from what you tell yourself, the audio tracks you continually play in your mind about your worth. The potential for a positive relationship begins within you and evolves as you learn to love, accept, and grow into who you are meant to be, for you, not for anyone else. Looking for others to validate who you are gives away your power and opportunities for creating and expanding your potential. When you stop looking for another person to complete you and let go of searching for a better half, you can begin to see yourself as a unique creation: a "you" that is evolving into the person who is ready to step into a mutually supportive and positive relationship.

Like Nahome, Jake, and Doug, I went through years of looking, seeking, and wanting a relationship. When I realized that all I was creating was a continuous cycle of looking and wanting, I had to shift my perspective from *needing* to *knowing* that I was worth the relationship I genuinely desired. I had to become clear on who I was as an individual and who I was as a partner. I realized that if I wanted a partner to complete me, I was accepting that I, on my own, was less than complete. Shifting from *needing* to *knowing* allowed me to clarify and affirm a partnership in which we do more than complete each other—we expand and create greater potential together.

The more I worked to expand my potential and accept my worth, the more I realized how complete I was as an individual. I stopped wanting, needing, and forcing relationships. I began to practice affirmations of gratitude for what I already had. Even though we had yet to meet, I knew the essence of my partner already existed.

This evolution happened while I was living in a small fishing village on the north shore of Tortola, British Virgin Islands. Each morning, I would wake up before dawn and be one of the numerous people walking up and down the steep five switchbacks of Windy Hill. As I walked, I repeated my mantra of gratitude for my yet-to-be-met partner. I began in November, and on January 6, at 5 p.m., I met Professor Alan, who had just arrived at my neighbor's home for the start of his six-month sabbatical.

Keep in mind; I am not writing the script for a new Disney movie. There was no immediate connection, no love at first sight or fireworks. Living in the village meant that we saw each other on a daily basis. We would say hello as we passed, exchanging pleasantries and the odd little chat. The chats grew into long conversations, during which we discovered how many similar interests and ideas we shared. We became friends and playmates, creating numerous island adventures. My feelings for Alan grew beyond friendship, and I realized that I wanted our relationship to continue past the ending of his sabbatical. Together, we discussed stepping into the risk of a committed relationship. He risked opening his life and home to me, and I risked leaving my new home and career in Tortola. Without risk, no loving relationship could evolve.

Our relationship continues to evolve to this day. It grows as we continuously and consciously strive to work at being the best we can be together. We ask the hard questions, risk sharing our deep feelings, and work through the messiness of misunderstandings. No magic, just commitment to our relationship as individuals and partners.

Relationships and Giving and Receiving

MORE relationships recognize that honoring others is a two-way process of giving and receiving. One cannot wholeheartedly give until one can also openly receive, nor can one truthfully receive unless one can also sincerely give. As with all aspects of MORE relationships, giving and receiving must begin with you. MORE requires that we give unconditionally, not needing, wishing, or desiring acknowledgment. The key word here is *unconditional*. It is giving from the heart and expecting nothing in return. Unconditional giving has a life force of its own. The gift comes from within.

I excelled as a giver. I gave to everyone; I prided myself on finding just the right gifts at just the right times. I gave unconditionally, or at least I thought I did. I am not sure how or when the insight hit me, but when it did, I was stunned. My giving did have conditions. Deflated by shame, guilt, and embarrassment, I realized that I was not giving as unconditionally as I had always proclaimed. I was in my thirties before I dug deep enough to accept that I did want something in return. I was looking for outside-in recognition, acknowledgment, and love. My giving was a subtle manipulation of others. A subconscious "How can you not love me? Look at everything I have given you."

To complicate matters more, it was not until I realized how conditional my giving was that I recognized that I was also a lousy receiver. I did not know how to receive openly. No one could give me just what I wanted; no one could equal my giving. That included both the tangible and intangible gifts. It was with the intangible gifts that my biggest opportunities came for learning and personal growth.

For years, I would not or could not accept a compliment or a thank you. I met any thank you or compliment with a comment that negated what was said. If I were told I looked good, I would deny it with some self-belittling remark. I responded to words of thanks for something I had done with comments like, "It was nothing." My responses immediately negated the gift of gratitude. No one could genuinely thank me, so why would they continue to try?

You all know people like this, and you may even be one of us. If you are, the shift is quite simple. Beginning today, every time you catch yourself about to negate an act of gratitude, just say thank you. Thank you for compliments, thank you for praise, thank you for other's recognition of you. Thank you. Allow yourself to feel gratitude, own your worth, and honor those who wish to thank you. It can feel uncomfortable and even emotional, and that is okay; go with it. Being uncomfortable and feeling your emotions allows relationships to grow. The more you practice and acknowledge gratitude, the easier and more comfortable it becomes. The more you own the emotions related to gratitude, the greater and more authentic your relationships.

> Grace is one of the "giver but not receiver" people. At the end of a coaching session, I asked her to take a few moments and tell herself, out loud, how proud she was of herself for the growth she had made and the changes

she had created for herself. Stunned, she was silent for a moment. "Okay, done," she responded.

"Grace, please say it out loud. See what that feels like."

She blushed, paused, and began. Her body language changed from arms crossed to arms open, head down to head up, and a frown to a grin. Acknowledging her growth allowed her to feel the pure power of giving and receiving. By the end of our session, she was giggling and very surprised at how the self-acknowledgment made her feel happy and proud.

MORE giving and receiving is a circular process; they feed into each other, and they feed our hearts. The results are always greater than the gift. Relationships come in all forms and sizes, from one-on-one to one-and-millions. Spreading unconditional love and kindness is infectious and soul building. Think of those random acts of kindness, from paying for the person's coffee in the line behind you to placing flowers on the desk of a colleague who needs a smile.

There is an incredible individual or group of people who have taken it upon themselves to make everyone's day, each day, just a little brighter. They are responsible for creating and placing random acts of art—colorful wooden sculptures of fish and sunbursts—on power poles all over the community. You see them, and you smile; it's that simple. No one knows who the mysterious artist or artists are. Social media has been abuzz with gratitude and appreciation, but no one has stepped forward to own it publically. These artists know that there is power in the MORE giving and receiving cycle—power to change a heart, a mind, and a community.

Relationships and Motivation

Every individual, in any relationship, has his or her agenda and core motivators. Each of us is driven and motivated by different stimuli. Some of us seek companionship and comfort; others thrive on power and prestige. People who flourish on independence and unpredictability can often find relationships challenging. Those who evaluate all relationships by equality and what they perceive as just can find relationships failing to meet their standards. Our core motivators complicate relationships further by operating at the subconscious level; they can vary from relationship to relationship and may change over time.

> Power and prestige are Dominic's drivers. As managing director, he has very specific professional goals and strategies for climbing the corporate ladder. In his estimation, striving to excel and be promoted is core to success. Miriam, one of his direct reports, totally frustrates Dominic with her desire to stay the course and maintain her current role and level of responsibilities. No amount of promotion carrots will entice her. She is exceedingly comfortable and competent in what she is doing, and she enjoys how she has integrated her job and her home life. Coming to terms with Miriam's perspective was challenging for Dominic, and while he says he accepts it, he still does not understand it.

As an educator, I always had complete control over how I taught my classes. The provincial government dictated the curriculum and objectives I had to meet, but I chose how to get there. I thrived on the flexibility and freedom I had, always adapting my teaching strategies and techniques, seeking to stretch and expand my students' learning and potential. My ideas and activities went beyond the classroom.

I created ways to take my students to the learning opportunities, not just present them with the words in books or questions on worksheets.

My need for individuality caused more than one relational conflict in my teaching career. If I felt my ideas were best for the students, I could not or would not see the situation from another perspective. I always pushed back and most often got my way, inflexible in my beliefs. In reflection, I now see that getting my way was at the detriment of a colleague, a student, or a friend. Hard, humiliating lessons to learn.

While individuality motivated my career, my love relationships were influenced by a need for companionship and comfort. Those motivations were generated by my lack of self-esteem and worth. I believed marriage would provide me with the comfort, companionship, and commitment I desired. I wished so much to be married that I made my first serious boyfriend's goals my own. I did whatever and went wherever he wanted to go and gave him the things that made him happy. The more I pursued his desires, the more I fed my insecurity metaphorically and physically. Deep down, I feared that if I did not go along with all his wants and needs, I would lose him and there would never be anyone else.

It was not until after we were married, when I lost weight and got fit, that I gained a new sense of self-confidence. My protective barrier removed, I began to do things for me, things that were important to me. The independence boosted my self-esteem and made me rethink who I was and what I wanted. Combinations of other life situations overlapped with my new perspective and led me to stretch my goals and life's desires. The more I pursued my goals, the less I was interested in his. Slowly, unknowingly, our lives began to journey down different paths. As I owned and fed off my inner motivations, I realized I was honoring my worth. Immersed in and inspired by my energies and passions, I missed looking up to see how they were impacting my relationship with my husband and our marriage.

Our relationship had begun based on my desire and need for comfort and companionship. Those desires, combined with the low sense of self-worth I had at the time, created a process that fostered a relationship that could only last as long as I negated my goals and desires. Once I discovered my passions, I was drawn away from the connection that had held my husband and me together. We had to go our separate ways. To be MORE, we each had to build a positive relationship with ourselves.

Knowing that each of us has different core motivators does not require that everyone end their relationships and go their own ways. Knowing your motivators can open the door for the creation of MORE relationships built on understanding your motivations and the motivations of your partner. That knowledge provides you both with an avenue for creating pathways to bridge your differences and build a MORE relationship that honors and respects the best in each person.

Relationships and Listening

Listening in a MORE relationship involves a focused speaker and a fully attentive listener. Focused and fully attentive means that neither the speaker nor the listener is multitasking—no televisions, no cooking, no cell phones, no computers, no other activity but speaking and listening. Our brains can only focus on one thing at a time. When you are "listening" to someone while in the midst of another activity, your brain has to jump back and forth between activity, listening and what you want to say in response. That means you are not entirely present. You are not fully engaged in the conversation. If a word or phrase has derailed your ability to

Lynda Reid, EdD, PCC

listen to the bigger message, apologize for interrupting and ask for clarification on what the person means by that word or phrase. Clarity fosters understanding; understanding builds relationships.

As you are reading this, if you find yourself saying, "I can multitask," think again. You will not have to dive deep into an online search to find the latest research on the negative impact of multitasking, which includes lowering your IQ and EQ (emotional intelligence), lessening your ability to organize and filter your thoughts, and decreasing the density of the area of your brain responsible for empathy and emotional control.

My first husband would think he was listening to what I wanted to say while he was watching television. When I called him on his split attention, he would mute the television and say, "Okay, now I'm listening" as he proceeded to watch the silent screen. The silent screen formed a barrier to our ability to share, listen, and understand.

Words themselves can also get in the way of understanding. Listening in MORE relationships requires the listener to listen beyond the words—to hear the feelings, the thoughts, and the baggage embedded in the conversation. Truly listening is not debating; it is not getting hung up on one word or how it is used. Doing so limits understanding and effective communication. If you get caught up and dwell on a particular word, you can miss the intent of what is being said and shut down the conversation.

We transmit a majority of our communication through our body language. MORE relationships pay attention to how others are looking, moving, sitting, or standing. We pick up clues of discomfort and stress from one's body position, cues that may not be communicated by the words one chooses. Arms crossed, head down, and a slouched posture convey a very different message from leaning forward, hands on hips, eyes ready for a stare down.

That said, it is important to note that certain body language directly connects to one's culture and beliefs. Eye contact, personal space, and crossing your legs can all be misunderstood from one cultural perspective to another. Such misunderstandings can block communication, damage relationships, and marginalize an individual or group. I have witnessed the destruction of a young man's self-concept by an authority figure in a school. The young man was being publicly reprimanded in the hallway outside a classroom. The teacher grabbed the young man's chin and pulled his face toward his screaming contorted face. "I said look at me! Show me some respect!" What the teacher did not realize was that, from the young man's cultural perspective, by diverting his eyes from the teacher, he *was* showing respect.

We live in a multicultural, global experience. We are all connected with, influenced by, and responsible to one another. Observing, respecting, and honoring differences is essential to the creation of MORE relationships. Through honoring differences, we can collectively own and create meaning.

I am a face-to-face person and honestly believe in the power and importance of body language. It was not until beginning my coach training and tele-classes that I truly developed my ability to "hear" body language, to listen to the unspoken text behind the words. When we actively listen, we become aware of each pause, breath, hesitation, and quaver in a person's voice. MORE relationships allow us to listen to, honor, and respond to all that is being said through the words, the body, and the energy of the speaker. We strive first to understand and clarify what is being said before responding and assuming we know the speaker's full intent.

> Daniel set a goal, which focused on fostering a more connected relationship with his wife. They are both extremely successful entrepreneurs, and

making time for each other was often a short-lived or random occurrence. Their conversations were short and incomplete, often creating tension and misunderstanding. They felt their lives and marriage drifting apart.

To honor each other and their desire to nurture their relationship, they made weekly dates, sometimes breakfast, sometimes dinner, and when possible, weekends. Their date time was a sacred time: no cell phones, no e-mail, and no interruptions. They took turns planning their dates and cherished the time they created to connect and truly listen to each other.

Relationships and Culture

Most of us live and work in multicultural environments. Even if we live and work in what appear to be very homogenous communities, we come from a unique combination of familial backgrounds, subcultures, and generational perspectives. Just because we look like someone else or someone from another group, that does not mean that we share the same norms, rituals, and belief systems.

Your culture is who you are; it is how you perceive and interact with others. Just as no other person thinks as you do, no other person will have the same cultural perspective as you. Living in MORE honors, respects, and expands our potential by seeking to understand and embrace our differences.

Kit moved from the United States for a job in the Caribbean. She assumed that as an African American, she would automatically be understood and accepted in her new job and African-based community. She was not ready for the relational boundaries and interpersonal tensions she encountered in the workplace. It was not until Kit began to share with me that the insight came to her. People were responding to her as an "American." Her skin color and cultural heritage had nothing to do with being accepted. She realized that she was behaving and interacting with her colleagues just as she did in the United States. Stepping back from her situation, Kit began to see and understand how others perceived her. Relationships and acceptance shifted as she worked to assimilate into the cultural norms of her new society. Assimilation became an avenue for respect and acceptance.

Moving to the Caribbean provided me with a similar opportunity. I learned very quickly that since I was not born there, I was not, nor ever would be, a belonger. My new neighbors stopped by to say hello and test my commitment to their village and island home. "How long you here for?" I was asked continually. I would have to explain that I had moved there and that I intended to make the island my home. Being a non-belonger, I consciously worked at observing, learning and practicing the cultural norms. It took time, but finally, I was accepted within the little fishing village in which I lived. I became what I refer to as an inside-outsider, the closest I would ever get to being a belonger.

Even within your own cultural context, relationships can be impacted by differences in sub-culture norms, values, and beliefs. I experienced the subtlety of subcultural difference between my family and my first husband's family. My family was controlled, polite, and considerate of visitors and friends. Guests to our home were always the center of our attention; we sought to make them as comfortable and happy as possible. His family, on the other hand, was open and rowdy; they took pleasure in making others feel uncomfortable and embarrassed. I first met his whole family at a dinner in his parents' home. Eight of us sat crammed around a large table in the small kitchen. Immediately off the kitchen, virtually beside the table, was the bathroom. Thankfully, I was not the first person to use the facilities. That lucky person would hear the loud, cheerful voice of his brother saying, "We can hear you! Can you hear us?" I was shocked into total bladder control, never using the bathroom in their home. It took me quite a while to let go of some of my more formal family norms and just relax with and enjoy being part of their family.

MORE relationships honor the fact that whether we travel to a new country, begin a new job, or become part of a new family, we all grow richer by understanding our differences. Embracing difference creates opportunities to expand the potential of all.

Relationships and Letting Go

No relationship is forever. People move, change, and pass away. Living in MORE acknowledges that all relationships, virtual and actual, are in our lives to support our learning and growth. Many of our relationships are passing; they change as we grow, age, and move on to new places, new careers, and new lifestyles. Others hang with you, compatible, supportive and evolving in parallel to you, fostering the best in both of you. Some relationships are leeches; they drain you, limit your growth, and negate who you are capable of becoming.

Social media has added a new public dimension to our relationships. The connectivity of the Internet allows us to reconnect with long lost friends and family and maintain these relationships over time and distance. Many of us have spent hours on various social media platforms searching, reconnecting, and compiling a friend list in the hundreds. What, when, and how our friends share can either enhance our relationships or deplete them. Social media allows us to publically "unfriend" people. We can use the protection of distance and our computers, tablets, or phone to publicly announce that we are removing anyone who "thinks like this" or "acts like that." Not that being more selective in the company we keep (online or in person) is not a suitable choice; it is the fact that we use a public platform to announce the removal of friends from our "lives." The virtual distance allows us a stronger voice and choice, or at least that is how it can appear.

Midway through his coaching series, Ty realized that he and his friends, people whom he had hung with since high school, had all become very cynical. Every time he was with them, their conversations would devolve into criticism, complaints, and negativity. In the past, Ty could hang with his mates for hours, leaving energized and happy. He did not know when or why he and his friends had all became complainers. They drained his energy and left him feeling frustrated and irritated. "I need to find new friends, but how do I let go of these guys?"

Ty toyed with telling them that they were all too negative and that he had better things to do with his time. He thought about just not answering their calls, unfriending them on Facebook, and just not seeing them, but how would he stop them from coming over to his place? "Perhaps I need to move?" he sarcastically joked.

The thought of blatant honesty did not sit well with Ty. He chose to slowly wean himself away from the group by immersing himself in new hobbies and interests, seeking out others of like energy and enthusiasm. Over time, the old group stopped calling and coming by his place. With new interests and friends, Ty found that his life grew fuller, more positively focused and energizing.

As I mentioned previously (under "Relationships and Motivation"), my first marriage began its decline when I began to embrace my self-worth and potential. I was oblivious to the impact that my choices were having on my husband. It was not until I returned from a summer trip that the result became apparent. Returning home, excited to reconnect, I was greeted with an emotionless statement: "At the end of the month, you can move out or I will." No explanation, no details, no conversation. I was devastated, shocked, and rocked to my core. We had been together for twelve years; how could this be happening?

Somehow, we managed to live in the same house for the next month, alternating who slept on the couch. We moved past each other in the mornings, no conversation, no words. We both stayed away from the house as long as possible in the evenings, only coming home to sleep. I packed up what was mine, and I moved back into my parents' home and tried picking up the pieces of my life.

Six months passed before I heard from my spouse. He was ready to talk, even to go to counseling. Surprised and confused by his sudden desire to communicate, I set up an appointment for both of us with a counselor. It was evident to me during the first session together that I needed time to reflect on and understand me before we could continue counseling as a couple. Through that process of counseling and self-reflection, I realized that I no longer was, or could be, the person he had married and that he was no longer the person with whom I could build the rest of my life. I could not go back; I had to move forward, and that meant divorce. Owning that realization and inevitability was extremely agonizing. I tortured myself back and forth with the intense pain of a love relationship that had run its course. I had to dig deep, honor my feelings, and let go. It was only through letting go that my husband and I were given an opportunity to move on, to become who we were each meant to be as individuals.

I have seen my ex-husband only a few times since our divorce, as our lives have taken each of us on very different paths. I will always love him for all we learned and created together and particularly what being with him taught me about myself. My past with him allowed me to learn what I needed to move my life forward. It was my first step toward understanding what I wanted to create in a committed relationship. Many people, like myself in my first marriage, find themselves in marriages that have hit dead ends. We married thinking our relationships were forever, not considering how we could each change and evolve on paths that would take us apart.

Some marry out of family and societal "must dos," not wanting to bring shame to the family or themselves. Culture, pregnancy, and age can all lead us down the aisle of regret.

> Sherie got pregnant when she was very young and married the father of her child, as her parents wanted her to do. When I began working with her, she felt depressed, worthless, and trapped. They lived in the same house but led separate lives. Their relationship was toxic and strained to the breaking point. She believed that since her actions had put her in this toxic relationship, this was where she needed to remain for the rest of her life.
>
> Shortly after she began coaching, Sherie and her husband went to couples counseling. Through coaching and counseling, Sherie began to explore and identify opportunities for her future. She realized that while she would never have a loving, intimate

relationship with her husband, she could create a positive change for herself and her son. She understood that even though she and her husband would no longer live together, they needed to learn how to coparent in a respectful and positive manner that supported their son. The shift took time, patience, and acceptance for both of them. Now, living apart, they are each becoming who they could not be together. By letting go of a relationship that would never work, they have created an environment for their son where he feels loved and supported by both of his parents.

Relationship and letting go take many forms in our lives, not just in our love relationships. Shifting out of our life's careers can lead us away from our identity and our place of meaning and belonging.

Retirement was a hugely anticipated transition for Iian. Retirement was the dream, his ultimate reward for a life of hard work. Now was time for the payback from forty-five years in the same career. Iian was seen as a leader in his field. Upon his retirement, everyone said how much he would be missed.

He stayed in contact with a few colleagues for a time. Others began to retire, and many moved away, resettling in warmer climes or immersing themselves into their families. Iian's closest relationships slowly disappeared; he felt alone, isolated in the city he had called home.

Loss of his professional self and status came as a surprise; he felt unsettled, empty, and no longer respected. He now has to rewrite who he is and who he wants to become. Iian is consciously seeking to develop new friendships and goals. He is working to identify the best of who he was professionally and entwine and honor it in creating the best of who he wants to be today.

While the loss of any close relationship requires you to move through your unique grief process, the ultimate in letting go comes with death. Death turns one's physical presence into a shell, the former home of one who was loved.

I missed the passing of my father by minutes. My plane was landing as he passed. His body, still in his bed, was warm; yet his essence, his spirit, was gone. I felt him nowhere and longed to be reconnected.

Every culture and every religion has a process of letting go and honoring the passing of a loved one. For each of us, death is a personal journey that takes time to comprehend and time from which to heal. Some of us share and process outwardly, while others shift inward for solace and healing. Whatever your process, honor it and the loved ones you have lost. Use their passing as a stimulus to honor the persons who have passed, build stronger bonds with those still with you, and become MORE of who you are meant to be.

MORE and Relationships

As with all aspects of MORE relationships, building strong, powerful, meaningful relationships begins with your relationship with yourself. Your worth and potential serve as filters through which relationships come into your life. Stepping into your worth and understanding your core motivators allow you to risk being accepted, acknowledged and loved. Being MORE permits you to practice gratitude by giving of yourself and receiving with openness and humility.

Meaning

Owning

Relationships

choice
unexpressed
wellness
forgiveness

Emotions

Blog Post: The Emotional Yo-Yo

I was a yo-yo flunky. Those two flat disks connected by a center axle looped in string were my bane. I was great at winding the string around the axle and throwing the yo-yo away from my hand, but having it return to my hand, let alone do tricks, was a frustrating challenge for me. Perhaps it was due to the size of my hand, my lack of eye-hand coordination, or the fact that I never persisted at perfecting my technique?

Learning to regulate my emotions was just as cumbersome. My emotional yo-yo responses were totally out of my control. At times, I let my emotion out without thought or consideration of whom it might impact. Other times, I kept my feelings tightly wound inside, afraid of judgment or rejection. As with my inability to control the little wooden yo-yo, I blamed other things. My feelings and lack of ability to honor and regulate my feelings were because of other people or events. "They" made me feel that way; "they" were the reason I could not express what I wanted to express. Worse yet, what would "they" think of me if they knew what I felt? It took me a long time before I realized I needed to own and take control of my emotional yo-yo.

No person or event "makes" you feel a certain way. Neuroscience has demonstrated that there is a fraction of a second between a stimulus and our brain's decision to make a response. It is within that fraction of time that we choose. Our first responses are based on our emotional triggers, the learned patterns of response we have developed over time.

Your positive emotions can open up your life, inspiring growth and goodness in others and yourself. Emotions such as happiness and joy are expansive and engaging. They open your circle of possibilities, fostering creativity and insight.

Emotions such as anger and fear close your mind down, limit your opportunities, and seek to hurt and to blame. Since our brains are hardwired to pay attention to the negative, it takes effort to stay within our closed mindset. The emotional yo-yo remains in the clenched hand, allowing the negative emotions to fester and feed on themselves. Left unchecked and misunderstood, these decaying emotions lash out, seeking revenge.

It takes courage and persistence to work with your emotional yo-yo, looking for safe ways to express your need to be heard. Fear and anger, just like love and joy, are all opportunities to explore and understand our emotional triggers. Once we learn the triggers, we learn when and how to choose our responses. We can regulate our emotional yo-yos. The more you practice emotional choice, the more you open yourself to understand and learn from others.

Emotions

The fourth core component of MORE is founded on understanding, honoring, and selectively choosing how you express your emotions. They are your personal barometer, signaling your innate response and trigger points to people and events. MORE emotions require you to understand and accept a few basic realities. First, no one "makes" you feel a certain way. How you feel is your choice. Second, when we stop ourselves from owning, safely expressing, and working through emotions such as guilt, anger, and pain, those emotions transform into dis-ease and disease in our bodies. Third, unexpressed emotions block your ability to create positive relationships and live fully MORE. Understanding, embracing, and working with your emotions can move you forward in the creation of meaning in your life.

Emotions and Choice

Neuroscience research using fMRIs (functional magnetic resonance machines), has demonstrated that our brains make decisions to move a fraction of a second before we are consciously aware that we will move. Within another fraction of a second, we become consciously aware of our choice to move. It is within that fraction of time that we can pause, breathe, and make a choice as to how we wish to respond in any situation. Our responses can either enhance or damage an occurrence or a relationship.

> Danielle's daughter, Kaylee, was a master at playing Danielle's emotional spectrum. Kaylee knew just how to get a reaction that she could use to her advantage. Danielle's reactions, usually anger and frustration, would always shut down their conversations, allowing Kaylee to storm away in disgust. These days, their conversations rarely got past the exchange of snarky

interactions and emotional outbursts. "Besides making you angry, what do you think Kaylee wants?" I asked.

"I don't know," admitted Danielle. The insight surprised her. She did not know what motivated her daughter.

That realization began to change the way Danielle perceived Kaylee's comments. By pausing and taking a breath, she started changing her responses from comments laced with anger and frustration to questions of interest and honesty. The questions led to further discussion, creating a deeper understanding and appreciation of each other. Their relationship transformed as they both felt heard, respected, and appreciated. They are on a journey toward MORE.

Misinterpreting the motivation of the other person, assuming we know why someone is responding as he/she is, definitely propels our responses to each other into the abyss of inappropriate emotional reactions. This includes the passive non-responses we use to control and manipulate others.

Richard was a master of the passive-aggressive response. It was his way of shutting down uncomfortable or frustrating situations. He saw it as "taking control." It was not until his new partner called him on his behavior that he realized how unconscious his passive aggressiveness had become.

In our coaching conversations, he began to explore alternative options for communicating when he was uncomfortable or frustrated. We role-played a few scenarios that triggered his passive aggressiveness.

The practice allowed him to work through his feelings in ways that supported conversation. Rather than shut people down with a comment and sarcasm that ended conversations, he sought to ask questions that demonstrated his interest and engagement in the thoughts and ideas of others. He began to grasp that much of his lack of comfort came from the assumptions he was making about the motivations of others, not from the actual situation. He realized that not only did he assume the motivations of others, but also, his passive-aggressive responses were related to his fear of being wrong or not having the right answer. Richard began to gain the confidence he needed to utilize new responses to uncomfortable situations with his partner, his friends, and his colleagues at work.

These were breakthrough insights for Richard. He realized he did not have to have the "right" answer, solve the problem, or fear sharing his feelings. His partner, coworkers, and friends were not testing him; they merely wanted his engagement and input into a situation. He shifted to viewing conversations as ways to creative avenues for new opportunities, instead of roadblocks and dead ends.

Many of our emotional reactions are learned responses we developed in childhood. Since our brains like to process events with the least amount of energy, old emotional triggers are our brains' go-to for responding.

Dareyl had lived in blame and anger since he was a young boy. Everyone—the entire world, it seemed— was always against him. His problems were never about him but about "them." It was because of others that he felt trapped in the depths of an anger pit. Dareyl's breakthrough came in the second half of his coaching series when he realized his anger was about himself, not others. He was choosing to live in an "anger pity party," and no one else could or wanted to attend. He decided that he wanted to risk being positive.

He began his journey toward positivity by practicing gratitude. At the end of each day, he would write down three things that he was grateful for that had occurred during the day. Things began to shift for Dareyl. Realizing that he could risk creating his happiness, he started to open up, to be vulnerable. Vulnerability, once impossible to consider, was now a ladder out of the anger pit, a ladder to new possibilities. He felt trepidation, but he was ready to climb out through his vulnerability, opening himself up to others. I loved the day he said, "If I risk being vulnerable, I won't have to be angry." The statement made him laugh, openly, honestly, and freely. Choosing to climb out of the darkness of his anger pity party, he embraced the light of new possibilities, new relationships, and a life of joy and harmony.

Emotions Unexpressed

I am not sure if it was because I was the middle of three sisters, but I grew up the pacifist, the one who never expressed my anger. My older and younger sisters could let loose on each other, from passive-aggressive combats to shouting matches. It was not until a counseling session much later in my life that the counselor asked me, "You've never expressed anger, have you?"

"No," I responded, not seeing that as any big deal. She explained that I still carried all that unexpressed anger within my body and it was limiting my health and personal growth.

She gave me an exercise to do when I was on my own, without any possible interruptions or time limits. I was to reflect on and write out every situation of anger in my entire life. The timing of the exercise could not have been more ideal.

It was Christmas holidays, and I was living with my sister, brother-in-law, and young nephews. My brother-in-law's parents were visiting, and they had all gone off to the mountains for a few nights. I organized my space and began to write, hesitantly at first, judging and questioning my memories. At some point, there was a shift, a transition. I wrote and wrote and wrote. Emotions rose. I yelled, screamed, and cried. Thoughts and feelings were scribbled across page after page until I was done, emotionally exhausted. Taking all the pages into the kitchen, cracking open the window above the sink, I began to burn page after page.

The weight of my exhaustion transitioned to humor and absurdity as the smoke alarm began to screech with the burning of every third page. With each shrill squeal, I took a tea towel and manically waved toward the high, out-of-reach alarm until it quieted. As the final pages turned to gentle fragments of ash, my vision was distracted by motion in the darkness outside. Two evergreen trees dropped over the back fence into the snow piled in the backyard. My sister's friend was delivering the Christmas trees they had cut down on his property on their way to the mountains. When I recounted this event to my counselor, she said, "That's fascinating. Do you know that evergreen trees are a sign of rebirth?"

Sign or no sign, the release of years of anger was a rebirth for me. I now know that to live MORE I need to honor and express my feelings, even anger. It does not mean I need to respond with yelling and screaming when someone triggers my anger. What I need is to let the other person, or people know how I feel by stating my feelings and my responses to the situation. By moving beyond blaming others for my emotions, I open the door for nurturing and growing relationships.

Acknowledging and owning my feelings allows me to create MORE relationships that are based on understanding, clarity, and acceptance. MORE relationships create a bond, a sense of belonging that creates meaning in my life. Notice how the components of MORE weave together, support each other, and expand our potential for creating harmony and fulfillment in our lives.

> I individually coached a married couple, Ted and Terrie. As all coaching conversations are based on confidentiality, what was said to me by one of them I never shared with the other. It was up to each of them to choose what and when to share their thoughts and insights with each other.

> Ted felt frustrated by his wife's inability to work through difficult issues. They had been together for years; he knew her history, her family. He blamed her problems on her dysfunctional upbringing. He labeled how she responded with "she always" and "she never." Ted thrived on solving problems and coming to a resolution. He prided himself on his abilities to push conflictive conversations to a solution and could not handle the fact that he could not do the same with her.

> Terrie feared conflictive situations and her emotions. When she felt herself becoming emotionally charged by a comment or question, she would shut down and

walk away. Terrie did not trust what she would say and how she would say things if she responded immediately to an emotionally charged situation. She needed time to withdraw, to process and think. Ted's need to push the conversation to immediate closure paralyzed her.

In time, as Ted continued to process Terrie's responses, he realized that his desire to push the conversation to closure meant that he was doing all the talking. He was never asking questions or listening to her needs. Even deeper, Ted realized that one of his motivations for doing so was his long-held fear of abandonment. He recognized that on an unconscious level, he feared that if she walked away, she might never come back. Closure was essential for survival.

They each, through their individual processes, realized that it was okay for Terrie to ask for time to process and work through her emotions, allowing her to say what she needed to say. Terrie began to gain the confidence to ask for the time she needed to process her thoughts and emotions so she could speak with honesty and respect, not from a place of threat and impulsive reaction. Accepting that she needed time allowed Ted to release his old fear of abandonment and provide Terrie with space she needed to process her emotions. They both committed to creating the time for the conversation to continue, permitting Terrie the opportunity to share her thoughts and feelings in ways that supported her growth and fostered the development of their MORE relationship.

The human virus state of overwhelm and stress plays havoc on our emotions and abilities to cope and function. Those of us who have experienced prolonged states of stress know very well the dark path down which it leads.

Jeanna lives in a state of overwhelm, professionally. As the vice president of a non-profit, she lives with constant change as every new initiative is added to her already-full plate. She finds herself wedged between the demands of the board, the expectations of the new president, and the frustration and complaints of her direct reports. The long-term stress is beginning to take its toll.

Jeanna came to coaching seeking a way out. She was disillusioned, emotionally battered and professionally devalued. Each time the president called her to come to his office, she was sure it would be her final day. The pressure was so intense that she feared she would lose control of her emotions, break into tears, and appear even weaker and more ineffective.

Our coaching conversations allowed Jeanna a safe space to release the overwhelmed emotions and to honor herself and her feelings. She began to reconnect with the old Jeanna, the successful, competent Jeanna. She started to own her worth, step back, and take a fresh look at her situation. As the weeks evolved, Jeanna realized that she was not just the "old Jeanna"; she was the new, evolved Jeanna. She chose to remove herself from the bonds of the professionally abusive situation. Jeanna's expanded outlook allowed her to see and create new possibilities for her future. A future that she creates, a future of living MORE.

Stepping away from toxic work situations can be scary. You are stepping into the unknown and trusting that you will create a more positive and purposeful future. Be wise, do your research, and know what you need to have in place to make this a successful step. I know many people who ironically have chosen not to take this step and found that their bosses made it for them. Those of us who have lived in overwhelm know the importance of stopping, taking stock, getting support, and taking actions that will reduce stress and create a positive direction forward.

Emotions and Wellness

When we are stuck in sadness, stress, and anger, our lives restrict; we draw into ourselves, closing down to new ideas or possibilities. Fed by the brain's natural tendency toward negativity, the negative emotions quickly fester and grow. Our energy constricts and goes to our body's core, triggering the fight-or-flight response. Cortisol, the stress hormone, is overproduced, killing brain cells. The response to stress and negative emotions creates sticky blood platelets, which can lead to heart attack and stroke.

Our wellness depends on our ability to recognize our emotions, where we are stuck, and why we are stuck, and to make choices to change. In the depths of our "stuckness," change may seem impossible, but change can and will happen. Slowly, one step at a time, when you are sick and tired of being sick and tired.

I have had clients who seek out coaching when they finally realize they are stuck; trapped in a web of disillusionment and shame.

> Vanessa is one such person. She had hinted at working with me for over a year. In her new role as general manager of a non-profit, she knew she had to make time for herself. Vanessa was ready to own her health,

restore relationships, and regain meaning in her life. Her goal process was positive and affirming, but she could not see a way forward. She committed an entire session to creating a strategy to gain control of her time and the frenzy of her work schedule. Her insights and actions for change gave her hope and physically began to melt away her stress and sense of overwhelm. She's ready to start change, one step at a time; a process of letting go and moving forward into her MORE.

When I was a teacher, many of my colleagues and I experienced the connection between emotions and illness throughout the school year. The start of the school year was a prime example. Inundated with a new curriculum, new classes, new students, and new expectations, many of us would get ill. The "teacher cold," we called it. "I caught it from my students. It's been going around the school." So complacent were we in expecting the inevitability of the "teacher cold" that we never stopped to consider that perhaps we had given it to ourselves. We failed to note how the stress of the new school year, the irritation with a particular student, or the frustration with developing a new curriculum was impacting our sleep and our health. At those times of high stress, we need to be even more vigilant toward our emotions and wellness, remembering to own our health.

I know busy, stressed-out professionals whose excuse for ignoring their emotional well-being is that they just do not have time. Funny thing about time and emotions—the longer you ignore that you are dwelling in the negative, the bigger the message your body will give. Teacher colds are nothing compared to heart disease, heart attacks, and strokes. Pay attention, read your emotional barometer, and note the growing pressure within. Act early; make time to relax, unwind, release, and sleep. Own your worth and your health. Book a massage, a pedicure, a spa day. Allow someone else to pamper you and nourish your cells. Pamper yourself; take a long bath with

Epsom salts or bubbles. "Pampering" oneself is not a gender thing. Everyone can benefit from making time to relax, release, and heal. Too touchy-feely for you? Then treat yourself to a funny movie. One that makes you laugh, really belly-laugh. Laughter is like an internal massage for your soul.

Happiness and laughter are expansive; they open us to the new, the positive, and unlimited possibilities. They are infectious and draw others toward us. As we share, we expand and evolve together. Happiness has been shown to release a range of hormones that aid the healthy functioning of our bodies, increasing memory, focus, and self-esteem. The hormone rush creates feelings of bliss, pleasure, and infatuation. Take a moment and go back to a situation when you were laughing hysterically. Close your eyes and relive the experience as clearly as possible. If you have allowed yourself to truly remember a situation, you will be smiling right now, possibly even having a silent chuckle.

My husband and I play a little game when we come across a server or a clerk who appears consumed in negativity. We like seeing how long it takes us to switch the negative energy to positive. We understand how easy it is for a person in a service industry to become stressed, overburdened, and frustrated. Customers can be demanding, unrealistic, and just plain rude. We begin shifting their energy by honoring who they are and connecting with them on a personal level. We ask for their advice and recommendation; we compliment them on their insights and personal qualities. Soon, we are laughing, smiling, and enjoying our time together.

We all appreciate being recognized for our work and efforts and feel a bond with those who understand and comment on the work we do. By acknowledging and understanding others, you are actively assisting in promoting their sense of health and well-being, as well as your own.

Laughter does not just promote good feelings and the reduction of stress; laughter also promotes health and healing. A good laugh triggers endorphins in our brains, activating our bodies' "feel good," pain-reducing chemicals. In 2007, my husband and I took humor and absurdity into his isolation room during his bone marrow transplant. We decided that the twenty-one days in his isolation room were not unlike going to space, so we decorated his room with posters of planets, galaxies, and nebulas. We gave science fiction names and titles to all the equipment attached to his body. We made videos of his "space" journey that perhaps one day we will edit and share with others. We amused all the staff, nurses, and doctors, which further fed our amusement. The staff loved coming into my husband's room. Through all his excruciating pain and endless hours tied to equipment, being awakened for blood draws at all hours of the night, my husband remained optimistic and confident. Laughter and humor helped him heal. Even the medical pros had to acknowledge the profoundly positive influence of our absurdity and humor. Laughter creates a foundation for wellness and living MORE.

Emotions and Forgiveness

We all carry emotional and perhaps physical wounds from others who have hurt us. Those individuals have broken our trust and crushed our beliefs in others.

> "But he wronged me! I'll never forgive!" Curtis stated emphatically. I asked Curtis if he had ever considered that by continuing to carry that wound, he was allowing that person to continue to control and wrong him. He had to take that thought with him for a while before he could fully process it and allow himself to forgive.

Forgiveness is not an instantaneous event. It is a thoughtful, conscious consideration and choice. In some cases, we cannot forgive a person to his or her face, but forgiveness consciously given allows us to release, rewrite, and move forward. Forgiveness is about opening the door of possibility, to owning your life, your worth. Through forgiveness, you take back your power and your control. Forgiveness allows you to make meaning from adversity and live a life of MORE unburdened by the past.

> The forgiveness idea intrigued Jason enough to send a follow-up e-mail to me regarding a presentation I had given to his class. He was particularly interested in self-forgiveness because he felt that it was a quality that he, others his age, and even people older than him did not practice. I responded to his e-mail, agreeing that forgiveness is a much-underrated yet powerful process and that many individuals do not know how to forgive themselves or others. I do not believe that you can forgive or love another until you can forgive and love yourself, and that you cannot truly forgive yourself unless you love yourself. Self-love is the doorway to self-forgiveness; self-forgiveness allows you to release mental baggage and beliefs that limit your potential. The process, "Love, forgive, let go, and grow," isn't easy, but it is essential. It takes continuous effort, self-awareness, and the ability to own your emotions and your worth; it takes living MORE.

Emotions and MORE

We all need to feel and experience the spectrum of emotions, from the negative to the positive. It is important for each of us to learn how and where to release the negative emotions in ways that honor our needs and promote growth and forward progress between ourselves and others.

MORE emotions acknowledge the science and power of positive emotions. They begin with your thoughts and center around what you say to yourself and how you speak to others. Placing your focus on the positive will create the positive. The MORE creates positive environments. Positive environments foster positive emotions, which increase your ability to solve problems, enhance your ability to think creatively, and increase your desire to collaborate with others.

The MORE

MORE acknowledges that we are human beings, not human doings. Well-being comes when you create a balance between your doing and your being. The MORE embraces the broader needs we all crave; it is not about merely putting smiles on our faces and pretending "everything is fine." It is about making conscious choices and taking concrete actions that support us mentally, physically, and spiritually. Those actions expand contentment and joy within our personal and professional lives. The support that creates meaning allows you to own your potential, foster positive relationships, and understand, respect, and work through the range of your emotions.

Just as my childhood friend, Karen, and I endeavored to create pixie dust, living MORE creates its own sense of magic—not Disney-ish, but the kind of magic that creates moments of tangible, genuine harmony and fulfillment. Living MORE allows you to explore the right combination of meaning, owning, relationships, and emotions, allowing you to sprinkle and share your gifts of love, understanding, compassion, and inspiration with others.

Enjoy your MORE.

Related Resources

The following resources are provided for you to further explore each component of MORE through the lens of other thought leaders, authors, and researchers. As with the examples given throughout the book, the resources listed may speak to more than one component of MORE. The following is by no means a complete listing, merely another step forward. Not all resources and the information they present will be appropriate or acceptable for every person. Find what resonates and supports your learning and growth. Create your ultimate MORE resource list by adding your favorites to the list.

Meaning

Chopra, Deepak

Like many of you, I first discovered Deepak Chopra's work in the late 1980s and early 1990s. *Unconditional Life* and *Quantum Healing* (Bantam Book, 1992) were two books that stretched my thinking, expanded my understanding, and challenged the way I perceived the world and myself. You will find that his work covers all the components of MORE. Visit Deepak Chopra's website, chopra.com, and explore the full range of his books, videos, and speaking schedule. You can also visit the Chopra Center for Meditation and explore the twenty-one-day guided meditations created with Oprah Winfrey. There may be one or more that speak to your needs.

Dalai Lama (His Holiness the Fourteenth Dalai Lama of Tibet)

The Dalai Lama's work transcends religious boundaries and speaks to every person. One of my favorite books of the Dalai Lama's is *An Open Heart: Practicing Compassion in Everyday Life* (Little, Brown, and Company, 2001). This book took me on an inward journey exploring my abilities to become more compassionate and develop a genuinely generous heart. His latest book, *The Book of Joy* (Penguin Random House, 2016), written with Archbishop Desmond Tutu, is a delight to read and contemplate. You do not have to be a Buddhist to appreciate the wisdom of the Dalai Lama; his books speak to the larger perspective of life. Visit his website, dalailama.com, and explore his biography, books, teachings, and messages.

Dyer, Dr. Wayne

Wayne Dyer has inspired thousands of people around the world as a motivational speaker and author. He is one of the few people I have met who can immediately fill a room with powerful, loving energy. The self-development and spiritual growth community felt a huge loss at his passing in August 2015. Fortunately for us, his work and words live on to inspire and teach ongoing generations. Explore Dr. Dyer's legacy at drwaynedyer.com, and find what speaks to you and your journey.

Frankl, Dr. Viktor

I first encountered the work of Dr. Viktor Frankl through his book, *Man's Search for Meaning* (Beacon Press, reprinted 1992). His work as a successful neurologist and psychiatrist was derailed by his incarceration in the Nazi concentration camp at Auschwitz during World War II. Visit the Viktor Frankl Institute, Vienna (viktorfrankl.org), and explore his books, videos, and theories. His words and work span decades, cultures, and countries. If you have difficulty navigating this site, you may find it easier to search for his books online.

Millman, Dan

In the 1990s, I had the incredible good fortune to attend one of Dan's Peaceful Warrior Intensives. It was the personal development course I refer to in the "Owning Your Failures" section, when I became acutely aware of the connection between mind, body, and spirit. More recently, I attended one of his lecture series at Omega Institute on the *Four Purposes of Life* (H. J. Krammer and New World Library, 2011). Dan Millman's website, peacefulwarrior.com, connects you to a range of his work from books, e-courses, and events. His peaceful warrior approach to living life wisely has inspired and guided people around the world.

Williamson, Marianne

Marianne Williamson is a spiritual author and lecturer. Her work, based on *A Course in Miracles,* illuminates the barriers that limit our potential. Marianne's early books, *Return to Love* (Harper Collins, 1992) and *A Woman's Worth* (Random House, 1993), expanded my understanding of spirit and helped move me forward in my life. Explore her books, blogs, courses, and videos at her website, marianne.com.

Owning

Brown, Brené

There is no shortage of Brené Brown's research and wisdom on vulnerability and shame, available online and in her books. Her honest, genuine approach draws you in and connects readers and viewers at a deeply personal level. One of the world's most-viewed TED talks is her *The Power of Vulnerability* (TEDx Houston, 2010). Explore her website and YouTube videos. There is something there for everyone.

Cain, Susan

In a world that promotes the extravert, Susan Cain brings meaning and focus to the power and strengths of being an introvert. Whether you consider yourself an introvert, extravert, or ambivert, you will find Susan's words and resources thought provoking and insightful. View her acclaimed TED talk *The Power of Introverts* and visit her website, quietrev.com, for further information and resources.

Cuddy, Dr. Amy

Like many, I discovered Amy Cuddy and her research on body language through her TED Talk, *Your Body Language Shapes Who You Are*. Her research has focused on discrimination, stereotyping, emotions, body language, and the effects of social interactions on our hormone levels. Her work demonstrates that we can use our body language to impact not only how others perceive us, but how we see ourselves. Find more about Amy and her work at amycuddy.com.

Hay, Louise

Louise Hay is a pioneer and leader in the alternative healing and positive psychology field. Her revolutionary book, *You Can Heal Your Life* (Hay House), was first published in 1984. This book transformed how I perceived the connection between my mind, body, and spirit. Louise has gone on to write numerous books, founding Hay House Publishing and Balboa Press. She lives what she teaches. Her website, louisehay.com, provides you with a broad range of resources and information.

Martinez, Dr. Mario

I was first introduced to the work and wisdom of Dr. Martinez through Dr. Christiane Northrup's book and online course, *Goddesses Never Age*. His theory of biocognition explores how our thoughts and our biology are intertwined with our cultural history. Through examining the connections within our lives, we can shift our thinking and improve our health and longevity. Find out more about his fascinating work at the Biocognitive Science Institute website, biocognitive.com, and read his book *The MindBody Code: How to Change the Beliefs that Limit Your Health, Longevity, and Success* (Sounds True, 2014).

Northrup, Dr. Christiane

As a woman, I was stunned by what I learned about my body when I read Dr. Northrup's first edition of her book *Women's Bodies, Women's Wisdom* (Bantam Books, 1994). Why had no one ever told us about our ever-changing bodies? Her work and her words have continued to inform and inspire me, most recently through her book and online course, *Goddesses Never Age* (Hay House, 2015). Explore Dr. Northrup's wide range of books and resources at her website, drnorthrup.com.

Seligman, Dr. Martin

A self-proclaimed pessimist, Dr. Seligman seems an unlikely person to be a pioneer in the field of positive psychology. As a psychologist, educator, and author, Dr. Seligman has researched, written, and spoken about the power of optimism and our abilities to learn optimism. His work has evolved from his 2002 book, *Authentic Happiness* (Free Press), to his books, *Learned Optimism* (Random House, 1991) and *Flourish* (Free Press, 2011). His work demonstrates that as we develop and practice optimism, we increase our health, vitality, and longevity. Explore his work at pursuit-of-happiness.org and at the University of Pennsylvania's site, authentichappiness.sas.upenn.edu.

Relationships

Bradberry, Dr. Travis

I first discovered Dr. Bradberry's work through his blog posts as a LinkedIn influencer. I always find his blog posts on emotional intelligence informative and insightful. He is the coauthor of *Emotional Intelligence 2.0* (Talent Smart, 2009) and the cofounder of the consulting firm, TalentSmart®, which provides emotional intelligence tests and training for Fortune 500 companies. You can find out more about Dr. Bradberry on his LinkedIn page, linkedin.

com/in/travisbradberry, and about his work on the TalentSmart website, talentsmart.com.

Covey, Dr. Stephen R.

Covey's *The Seven Habits of Highly Successful People* (Simon and Schuster, 1989) brought principle-centered personal development into the workplace. The structure of the seven habits focuses on examining ourselves as individuals before exploring our interrelatedness with others—the personal before interpersonal. His work is timeless and may even speak to us more today than it did at the time of its first publication. You can discover his "habits" and more of his work at stephencovey.com.

Covey, Stephen M. R.

Stephen M. R. Covey's best-selling book *The Speed of Trust* (Free Press, 2006), moved trust from a soft skill that is nice to have to an essential, measurable, hard skill that builds organizational effectiveness and profits. Building trust is an essential in all successful relationships. Explore his work and resources at speedoftrust.com.

Goldman, Daniel

Goldman shares his research, insights, and applications of emotional intelligence and social intelligence through his blogs and books, as well as in the development of personal and leadership potential. His research, work, and insights are structured to guide and stretch each of us personally and professionally, in increasing our capacity to connect, understand, work, and learn with one another. Visit the range of his work at his website, danielgoldman.info.

Rock, Dr. David

I was fortunate to have David as a trainer for two of my initial coaching/training programs with his then-titled Results Coaching System. His books, *Quiet Leadership* (Harper Collins, 2006) and *Your Brain at Work* (Harper Collins, 2009), expanded my thinking about how and why we listen to, think about, and respond to others. Dr. Rock is director of the NeuroLeadership Institute, which blends the latest in leadership and neuroscience findings into cutting-edge leadership programs. Learn more about his work at davidrock.net.

Emotions

As all the components of MORE weave together to impact and expand each other, you will find that the work of the majority of my references also speaks to the MORE component of emotions. These include thought leaders and researchers such as the following:

Brown, Brené
Bradberry, Dr. Travis
Goldman, Daniel
Hay, Louise
Martinez, Dr. Mario
Northrup, Dr. Christiane
Seligman, Dr. Martin
Rock, Dr. David

One additional resource I would like to mention here is Shawn Achor. Shawn is one of the leading world experts on the connection between success and happiness. His research on happiness has led him from Harvard University to the creation of the happiness consulting firm GoodThink and the Institute of Applied Positive Research (IAPR). His talks draw you in with gentle humor, genuine honesty, and extensive knowledge. Explore his books, presentations, and courses at shawnachor.com.

About the Author

Dr. Reid's eclectic career has always been driven by her passion to guide people in enhancing their lives' evolution. This passion has led her to explore a great diversity of roles in a wide range of locations. Her teaching, coaching, and consulting career began in Edmonton, Alberta, Canada, and has moved her back and forth through the Caribbean, the United States, and China. Those journeys inspired and guided her master's thesis and doctoral dissertation on the importance of cultural immersion and the development of multicultural leadership.

Dr. Reid states, "Some might say that change is my muse. I thrive by stretching my creative and intellectual abilities to inspire, engage, and expand individual and team potential. My 'go-tos' are the latest in the neuroscience of coaching, talent development, change management, multicultural leadership, cultural competency, humor, mindfulness, and work-life harmony."

Currently, she operates her own coaching business (Kusala LLC) in the British Virgin Islands and the United States. Her clients include individuals seeking change, budding entrepreneurs, and senior management in a wide range of professions. These clients all share the desire to break beyond the status quo and maximize their individual and group potential.

Printed in the United States
By Bookmasters